a view from the deck

my christian journey
with same-sex attraction

by rob farnsley

A View From the Deck
My Christian Journey With Same-Sex Attraction

Copyright 2015 by Rob Farnsley

Edited by Jerry Guibor

Contents

Endorsements

In my work as a pastor, I often tell folks two things. One, every story is a gift. Two, we're only as sick as our secrets. I've known Rob as a close friend for over twenty years. It has been my double privilege to serve as his pastor for much of the time. I commend his story as a gift on many levels. By telling his unique story, not only has he gotten healing grace from Jesus in his own life; he has made possible for other individuals to experience the same by bringing their own struggles into the light. As a bonus, he has helped put a greater degree of grace into Orlando Grace Church. My prayer is his book will do the same for many other churches as well.

— *Curt Heffelfinger*
Pastor of Orlando Grace Church

It's been said everyone has a book within them waiting to be written. Rob Farnsley could wait no longer and took the courageous step of writing his story, revealing the big secret he hid for many years, together with the redemption that followed. It is a story filled with hope that even if the worst about us becomes known, God is still our biggest cheerleader and will use the worst about us to reveal the best about Him.

— *John Certalic*
executive director of Caring for Others, inc.

Few men truly inspire. Even fewer truly listen. Having had the pleasure of knowing Rob for several years, I have experienced firsthand the inspiration he has given many by truly listening to our hearts and inspiring us to approach life with strength and love. The view from Rob's deck is a perspective worth knowing, a glimpse into the life of a man who has captured the essence of Jesus' ministry by investing in people. I'm thankful for his continual "giving of courage" to trust completely that we are the apple of God's eye and I'm even more thankful to be a part of his story.

— Adam E Wainio
Small Business Owner and Entrepreneur

Acknowledgements

THIS BOOK HAS BEEN ALMOST 70 years in the making. It is my autobiography. It deals with with my same-sex attraction issue and how I dealt with it over the years. It is not a treatise on same-sex attraction (SSA). I don't make judgments as to it being right or wrong, Biblical or not, and so on. It is an attempt to help the church, the body of Christ, be more honest and safe for us to deal with the deep seated issues we have without fear.

There are many to thank. Adam and Bethany, who first helped me get started on this, and spent many hours with me. Jerry, who volunteered his expertise in editing and continuing the writing. He kept me on track. Those who read the manuscript and helped make things flow better. A host of others who have cheered me on along the way. For fear of offending those I might leave out, I won't mention any more names. You know who you are and I am forever thankful for you all.

Foreword

Rob Farnsley (we used to call him "Bob," and I still can't get used to "Rob"; "What about Bob?" sounds so much better than "What about Rob?") is very, very special to me. Of course, one reason for this is that we have been friends for 37 years. But there is another reason that towers over all others. In 1968, I was in my junior year as a chemistry major at the University of Missouri, and Rob was a staff member at Mizzou with Campus Crusade for Christ. Well, in late October he came with a team to talk about Jesus to my fraternity house, Sigma Alpha Epsilon. I was interested but not convinced, so Rob and I met weekly for about a month. He answered my questions and loved me as a brother. Finally, in late November, I gave my life to Jesus, and it was the greatest decision I ever made. For the next 18 months, Rob discipled, mentored, and cared for me as a father would his own child. Rob's passion for Jesus, his love for people, and his unwavering commitment to the Great Commission were important factors that moved me to go into the ministry upon graduation. Once I serendipitously walked by Rob on campus while he was talking to another student who, I found out later, was telling Rob that he no longer was interested in growing in Christ. After the student left, Rob took me into the chapel, sat down, and wept for a long time. I had never seen anything like that before, especially given the complete superficiality of the guys in my fraternity. I said to myself, If this is what Christianity is about, count me in all the way!

A few years after graduation in 1970, Rob and I drifted apart. Not because of any tension in our relationship. It was because we lived thousands of miles apart from each other and never ran across each other's path. Our friendship was still there; we just didn't get many opportunities to renew it.

What Rob shares about himself in this book was new to me when he told me about it around a year before the book's publication. What struck me when he told me was that I experienced in him the same old integrity I had seen in the late 1960s. He said he had lived a celibate lifestyle, that neither he nor the book was a crusade to change church doctrine (he still holds traditional views about homosexuality and gay marriage), but that he had experienced the church to be a very unsafe place to open up, talk about deep life issues and struggles, and receive help, love, admonishment, and encouragement from brothers and sisters. I believe everything Rob told me to be the sober truth.

It took guts for him to write this book. Why? Because he will draw fire from those on the extreme right and left. But this was a book that needed to be written, and Rob knew it. Like the man I have always known, he tries to do the right thing when he is convinced that it is, indeed, right. And I agree with his decision to put his story and concerns on paper. As Rob tells the story of his life, he has one and, as far as I can tell, only one agenda: to challenge the church to be a safer place where people can go deep, open up, and share what is really going on inside of them, including their dark side, and receive love, care, help, and the other "one anothers" of Scripture, all of which lead to repentance where needed, and to Christ-like Christian maturity under the authority of the Bible.

I have never read a book with which I agreed 100 percent, including the Bible! I often have to struggle with it until I finally come around and regain my senses! In fact, I agree with only about 75 percent of the books I have written! So it is likely that you will find things in this book with which you disagree. But, of course, that is part of the book's message – when that happens, the church ought to be a safe place to talk about disagreements in a spirit of love and safety, and with a view toward getting at the truth. I am proud of Rob for writing this, and I am grateful to you for reading it.

— JP Moreland
February 2015

Preface

It was the best of times, it was the worst of times, it was the age of wisdom, it was the age of foolishness, it was the epoch of belief, it was the epoch of incredulity, it was the season of Light, it was the season of Darkness, it was the spring of hope, it was the winter of despair, we had everything before us, we had nothing before us, we were all going direct to Heaven, we were all going direct the other way – in short, the period was so far like the present period, that some of its noisiest authorities insisted on its being received, for good or for evil, in the superlative degree of comparison only.

– *A Tale of Two Cities,* Charles Dickens

I LIVE ON A DECK. Well, I don't actually live ON a deck. I live in a mobile home that has a good-sized deck in front, looking out over a lovely view of the lake on which I live. I love this place.

When I first moved here from overseas, I needed a place to live. I had returned from my 11 years overseas with an international mission agency to join what its headquarters called the "Member Care" team. There was a campground on the mission property, and there were also a few mobile homes on the property.

I was taken to a vacant one that the main office was thinking of pulling out so it could rent the space to an RV owner. It was a single-wide with one small bedroom, not too large on the inside, with a sun room running the length of the mobile home. It was next to the water, with a deck looking over the lake.

As soon as I saw it, I said, yes, I think I can handle this place. I could walk to and from work from there and come home for lunch.

After I moved in, I tore out the raunchy carpet, put in some cheap laminate flooring, installed some new windows in the front, and doubled the size of the deck, which runs across the whole front of the mobile, about 20 feet. If you step down from the deck and walk across about 10 feet of grass, you are at the lake.

Over the last eight years, "the deck," as it became known, has become a place, a refuge, an idea, a memory, and probably lots more. I refer to living on the deck, or life on the deck.

I invited people to the deck, and over time the deck became a place where one came for "deck therapy." I have a new Website, *www.decktherapy.com*, and you may want to go to it.

Through the first six years, life on the deck was the greatest thing ever. I have a good friend, who observed my life, and he said, "Rob, I think you are the happiest man I know." I think it was true. I was really happy. In fact, he labeled me the "HMOE." The Happiest Man on Earth. I liked being the HMOE. It was the best of times.

But I am not the HMOE anymore. My "H" – my "happiness" – came to a crashing halt in 2012. What Job says in Chapter 3, Verse 25 became true for me – "What I feared has come upon me: what I dreaded has happened to me."

The secret that I had carried for most of my 66 years came out. I admitted I struggled with SSA – same-sex attraction. While it was terribly shameful and a huge monster hiding inside me, those weren't the worst parts of the fear. What I really feared was that I would lose my friends and their respect, and also my job. Much of my adult life had been spent working full time in various Christian organizations of the conservative, evangelical kind, in the type of jobs that require raising financial support. How could one carry such a secret, as I did, and continue to be upright and forthright with a mission agency, a supporting church, and supporters and friends? Especially if the secret came out.

This book will deal with all this, along with the rest of the amazing life I have lived and am still living. It is MY view from the deck. Some of it will deal with SSA. Much will not. I am not advocating gay marriage. I have no agenda regarding any of those hot issues. It is my life story, the good and the not-so-good – the duality and the duplicity

– and a story that I never thought I would write about, because I never thought my secret would come out.

Thank you for reading my story. My prayer is that it will help all of us in dealing with SSA issues, and a host of other issues that people – whether inside the church or not – are too afraid to talk about. Along with that, I hope it helps to create some safety and honesty within the body of Christ.

So let's start with how my world came crashing down. It was the worst of times.

Chapter One

Revelation of the Secret

"Most people live with a subtle dread that one day they will be discovered for who they really are and the world will be appalled."

— *The Sacred Romance,* Brent Curtis and John Eldredge

WHERE IN THE WORLD DID I put that thumb drive?" I wondered. I looked between the seats of the borrowed car I was driving. I searched through the house where I was staying. I rummaged through my luggage that was packed and ready for my return to my home on the east coast. I had to find it. By now, my search had stretched over several days, and I was alternating between frantic and hopeful, that it had been lost for good.

Sure, it didn't have important things on it, and thumb drives with enormous capacities have dropped precipitously in price. So cost wasn't the issue. But there were some things important on it that mattered only to me, as harmless as they seemed.

The fact is, they were photos I secretly carried on trips.

I wracked my brain, trying to think if there was anything "incriminating" to me on them. I decided there was not. Nor did I think that there was anything that would link them to me.

"OK," I continued my self-talk, "maybe I'll find the thumb drive later – if it isn't lost forever, and that would be fine with me."

A thought began to nag at me: "Could I have dropped it somewhere at the church?" It was early in the morning during Easter week, and I had just returned from the 6 a.m. men's Bible study. I raced back to the Bible study room at the church to see whether I might find it. There was only a janitor who had seen nothing. So, I guessed I had not lost it there. I retraced every step from the car to the room, hoping to see it. Nothing. Oh, where could that thumb drive be?

***

It was the spring of 2012, and I had spent a few weeks in Fresno, California, where I had lived for many years before leaving in 1991 to embark as a missionary. Although I had had a long history of Christian outreach on college campuses, and then at my church, becoming a missionary was a hard step that was filled with trepidation, joy, excitement, and great agony.

After about 10 years in the real estate business, around age 45, I was wrestling with what I was to do with the life I still had before me. I had read a book, "The Man in the Mirror," and it had a huge impact on me. In one chapter the author, Patrick Morley, writes about having a life-purpose statement and the need to put it in writing, on paper, in black and white. Most people around me thought my life was very purposeful, but somehow I was captured by this idea. I eventually came up with a life-purpose statement. I did this by attending a weekend retreat with Randy, a young man I was discipling, at his cabin in Yosemite. We went for this express purpose. Thank you, Randy! I came away from that time with my life-purpose statement: "We proclaim him, admonishing and teaching everyone with all wisdom so that we may present everyone perfect in Christ. To this end I labor, struggling with all his energy, which so powerfully works in me." Colossians 1: 28-29.

Some years passed, and I came across John 4:34, which I had read many times. Jesus is speaking: "My food is to do the will of Him Who sent me, and to finish His work." The verse may not be as direct a challenge as the Great Commission in Mathew 28:19, which says: "Go ye therefore, and teach all nations, baptizing them in the name of the Father, and of the Son, and of the Holy Ghost."[1] But, given the spiritual experiences and understanding I had gained in the previous few years, I knew that, if I were to write this in my Bible as my current

---

1. King James Version

life purpose (it can change), there would be a major upheaval in my life. Explicit in the verse is finishing His work, and to me, that meant becoming a missionary. Frankly, I did not have the highest regard for missionaries, let alone becoming one.

In 1989, I got my first taste of missionary work by going on a short-term mission trip to what we called Borneo in those days. Today, it is Kalimantan, a part of Indonesia, across the South China Sea from Singapore.

First, I followed around a tireless man, Bob Williams, through the jungles of Borneo. He and his wife first arrived as missionaries to headhunters who had never seen a white person, in the late 1930s. Five decades later, their influence could be seen in little churches scattered throughout the island, living testimonies to their legacy. By the time I went, Bob and his wife were elderly, and they had settled in Fresno, but he was returning a few times a year.

While there, I met very talented people – humble missionaries – who could have done very well financially in this world. Instead, they had given everything up for the sake of giving all people the opportunity to hear the good news of Jesus Christ. Some confessed their fears to me that they were not sure what would happen to them when they got older. They were not buying houses back in the States or Canada, and had very little put away for retirement.

My regard for missionaries was changed significantly by these two examples. These were not people who couldn't do anything else. These were intelligent, young, gifted people who could have succeeded in various occupations in life. They had given up everything for this endeavor and I admired them for it. It brought me to tears as I was leaving. I remember clearly sharing with one of them, through my tears as we walked to the airstrip where our little plane was waiting. What was I to do with my life? He didn't pressure me to come. He simply said that God would direct my path. Pray.

When I returned to Fresno, I told my pastor at the time that we needed a mission committee at our church. We needed to become more aware of the foreign mission field. Our church supported many workers overseas, but most of these were people he had met and pledged our support to. They were not people from our church. Nor were our people very aware of who these people were or what they were doing. Nor were we aware, other than vaguely, of the needs of those overseas who had no opportunity to hear the gospel. His response, in his booming voice, was something like this: "Fine, Farns. You want a committee for missions? YOU do it. No one on our staff wants another job." So, I did. Then, a class called "Perspectives on the World Christian Movement" came along. It also had a huge effect on me. Just as the name says, it gave me a perspective of what God was doing in the world. I was amazed at the people who went and what they were doing. I read a lot of biographies at that time. I also became more aware of what still needed to be done. Still, I did not see myself as a "goer." I was content to be a "sender." As usual, God had other things in mind that I didn't.

After months of praying and talking to those close to me, in August 1990, at Lake Tahoe where I went every year, I changed my written life purpose to John 4:34. It confirmed what I already knew – regardless of my intentions – that going as a missionary was the only way I could "help" finish His work. But how and to where?

Five months later, my house was rented, and almost all of my possessions were sold and the remainder given away. All debts were paid. I was on my way – first to Indonesia and then Bosnia as a missionary.

**

Over parts of the next 20 years, I returned regularly to Fresno to visit long-time friends, supporters and donors, and of course my church. Now, I was visiting again. Although I did not know the new pastor well, he was very supportive of me.

During the Easter week of 2012, the church was holding early morning prayer walks around the campus. I attended several of them, and on this last day in Fresno before leaving for home in the east, I went one more time. I arrived at the prayer vigil with time to spare. When it ended, I stood to leave and meet old friends for breakfast before my flight. An elder in the church stopped me and said that the pastor wanted to meet with me. Nothing unusual about that, I thought. I had time to cancel my breakfast engagement and headed to his office in the main building.

When I entered his office, I was surprised to see two other leaders in the church. It immediately struck me that something was not right. I wondered: "What is this all about?" Nothing like this had happened to me before. It was as if I had been told to report to the principal's office and the entire school board was waiting there, ready to suspend me for some egregious infraction.

My heart started to pound a bit harder. We sat down.

"Do you have anything you want to share with us?" the pastor asked.

What could I say? I had two seconds to think it over.

Fear suddenly gripped me by the throat. My stomach knotted up. Had they found those pictures? I did not know. What if they had? Did anything point to me? If I didn't think so, I could deny it. With my whole life racing before my eyes, not to mention my heart, and my future life looking dim and probably over, I knew what I needed to do.

I said, "Yes."

What a relief to do that. Something I thought I would never do, or even be asked. I let it out. Regardless of what the future held. And it did not seem that the future held much.

I then told them an abbreviated version of my life story – the secret that I had carried all those years. They were so graceful and they cared for me, I could tell. At the same time, they thought that I needed to notify my mission agency's office. I did right then from the pastor's office. At the end, we destroyed those pictures on the thumb drive together.

***

My view through the years was that the pictures I had on the thumb drive were not "bad" pictures. They were like those anyone can see on packages of Hanes underwear at a department store, or similar pictures. They were not pornographic, in my mind. But they were arousing to me. In that sense, I think they were pornographic.

Over the years, I got a lot of mileage out of the idea that I was not attracted to pornography and, therefore, I was OK. But I guess one could say that, if anything turns you on in an arousing way, it is pornographic. My fantasy was not to have sex with these pictures. I just looked, got aroused, and did "act out." I never in my life pursued sexual involvement with another man. That lifestyle was not appealing to me and, of course, it would have been a disaster if I ever did that. But I never did.

I used the line of thinking that I think many men do, regardless of what they are looking at. "I'm not hurting anyone. It is just me and a picture. Lots of men do far worse stuff."

***

I hardly got out of the pastor's office before getting a text message from a close friend asking me whether I was OK. How did he already know? I assured him I was, that there was just some mission-related stuff I needed to discuss with the pastor.

How did he know, I wondered? Where is there any safety in this world? Not even in a pastor's office? I later found out how the word might have spread, but I must say I'm a bit skeptical about being able to have confidentiality within the church. Too many eyes and ears, and too many revealing "prayer requests."

***

The flight that day back to my home on the east coast was personally a rough and bumpy ride. If there ever had been a time I wished a plane, with me in it, would go down, it was then. Not that I was willing to make it happen myself. But I thought I might sing the "Hallelujah Chorus"[2] if we were going down.

A friend and colleague met me at the airport and spent the night with me. I think there was concern as to what I might do to myself. The next morning I met with the leaders of the Member Care team (of which I was a key part) and told them the story. This was followed in the next days with more meetings with the upper leadership in the mission agency – people I had known for many years. After those meetings, I went to see my pastor here in Orlando, who is also a close personal friend, and tell him.

It was a shameful time. I am not ashamed any more of who I am. Well, maybe I still struggle with it a bit. But I sure was then. I also was afraid, almost certain, that it would cause me to lose my job and standing in the mission organization.

It was a very unsettled time in our office over the next weeks. I was relieved of doing any ministry duties. However, I was still around, doing mundane things, and leaving almost daily for counseling meetings of one sort or another. In time, people were wondering, I

2. The "Hallelujah Chorus" is the climactic ending of George Frideric Handel's *Messiah*, composed in 1741.

think, if I had cancer or some other horrible disease. Eventually, I had a meeting with only my teammates on the Member Care team (not the entire mission agency) and told them my story. I asked for their forgiveness for being deceitful all these years. I received a lot of forgiveness and support, love, respect, affirmations. I heard words like "you'll come back and be better than ever." I did come back, but not to rejoin the team. That never happened. Even though I think I am "better than ever"! Certainly, I am more open and honest than ever.

Why was I ever closed and deceitful in the first place?

Chapter Two

My Years Growing Up

"As I think back on my childhood, the word shame serves as an umbrella. It is the sense of being completely insufficient as a person, the nagging feeling that for some reason you're defective and unworthy." — Brennan Manning, *All is Grace*

WHY AM I SO SCREWED UP?" Or maybe it would be better for me to ask, "Why I am so screwed up in the male/female dynamic?"

At least part of the reason, and pretty big, I think, is the image I have of parental love for one another that I saw over my childhood.

Or didn't see.

For me, the seminal picture of my childhood, and parental love for each other, was this scenario:

It's 5:30 in the evening. I am sitting at the kitchen table watching Mom fix dinner. Dad comes home, sets his lunch box on the counter, and turns around to give Mom a kiss. She stands there, hands to her side, and lets him kiss her a few times, but there is no response on her part.

I call it kissing a cold fish. That's what physical love is to me . . . kissing a cold fish. For me, it goes both ways. Even though I admit to my SSA, it's not as if I would like to do that with a man either. The whole picture to me is just not appealing.

Oh, I like hugs for sure. I want to be hugged, and sort of have a reputation of cracking the backs of guys when I give them hugs. I like kissing little kids on the top of their head, holding babies (a little), and giving them that loving kiss that people do. I like that. However, I am still like a kid at the movies who, when a love scene comes on, turns his head and says, "Tell me when it's over." I love touch and, again, I love to be hugged.

I stand and cheer every time I read or hear a line from John Eldredge (probably in several of his books), which, I am sure, many others have written as well. It is this: "The best thing parents can do for their children as they grow up is to let their children see them physically love one another." I often wonder how I might have turned out differently if I had seen that. I long to have seen that. If nothing else, it might have helped me enjoy love scenes in the movies.

***

When did I first realize I had same-sex attraction? My earliest recollection of this is when I was about 6 or 7. I remember looking at the Sunday comic section and the picture story of Prince Valiant. I looked at the pictures of him and fondled myself. I don't think at the time that I thought anything about it other than the fondling part. My friends were calling me to come out, and I could not stop the fondling. When I finally was able to stop, I left. Again, I don't think at that time being aroused by those pictures was disturbing to me at all. What I had to hide was the fondling.

I don't remember same-sex attraction ever being discussed when I was young. I don't know if I even knew what that meant. At least in the earliest years. At some point, I understood the word "faggot" and used it myself in reference to others. Whatever I may have suspected about myself, it became more and more important that I keep it secret.

I discuss in other places my desires to get married. I always thought I would, until about age 46. So I was never ready to admit that I was a homosexual. Or that I struggled with it. Whatever I was, I also knew I did not desire to live a married life with a man. And that brings me back to the "seminal picture" I was describing.

***

My mom was a pretty lady. About 5 feet, 3 inches tall. Brunette. Not skinny, but not overweight. Just right. And Dad probably wasn't bad either. He had a ruddy complexion, as do I, and I don't like it. Sunburning so easily. I am not attracted, if that is the word, to men who are like me.

He was just under 6 feet. Maybe about 170 or 180 pounds. He seemed to be in good physical shape. Mom admitted (both are long since passed away) that she did not love my dad and, I guess, never did. I think he was madly in love with her. It was the end of World War II, and I think Mom was not sure, being from a very rural area, that she would find anyone. Who knows? She may have been swept off her feet for a short while. Dad may have looked great in his Army uniform at the USO dances. I have heard more than once that he was a charming guy in those days. But as I grew up, the love was gone.

If I had the chance to be with both of them and had one question to ask each, it would be:

Dad, what was it like to be married to a woman you knew didn't love you?

Mom, why did you marry Dad if you didn't love him?

Of course, I am thankful they did marry, as I am a product of it. Screwed up though I may be. I say that facetiously. I am thankful for who I am now, and do not think I am "screwed up."

Mom's parents came to the United States from Slovakia around 1920. Some of the children were born in Slovakia, and the rest around Superior, Wyoming, not far from Rock Springs. The family was large and Catholic. Mom was one of the youngest of many girls and a couple of brothers. More than 10 of them, I think. Her dad, my grandfather whom I never knew, worked in the coal mines in Superior, and they lived in one of the small wood frame houses provided by the company. As I remember, it was called "D" Camp. Superior is basically a ghost town now.

Mom was the first of the children to graduate from college, the University of Wyoming. She went into elementary teaching. Mom died in 1976 at age 60, when I was 31. Many of her sisters had passed away by then. Cancer was a big killer in her family. It causes one to wonder what at "D" Camp, over the years, might have contributed. Maybe it was a pall of coal smoke that hung over the camp, although in windswept Wyoming it is hard to imagine a pall of anything lasting long in the air without being blown away.

Dad's roots go further back in U.S. history. I have always referred to my bloodline from his side of the family as a "Heinz 57" variety, mainly English, Scotch, Irish and probably some German.

At any rate, that makes me half Slovak. I like that. It makes me feel a bit rooted in a place that I can identify. In 2005, I was able to visit the village where my grandparents lived before they left to come to America. It was a summer's day, and everything was green and beautiful. It was in a wooded area, and quite lovely. When I thought of my grandparents leaving this place for bleak, windswept, dry, desert-like, cold Wyoming, it seemed to me that they must have sat and cried on the steps of their little house in "D" Camp as they missed the "old country."

My growing understanding of my roots gave me one more nail to hammer in my father/issue coffin. Mom had roots, bleak and poor though they were. What did Dad give me? Some mixture of who knows what, along with the half-Slovak side my mom gave me. That sounds pretty harsh, and it sure wasn't his fault. I just wanted to feel like I was somebody, and my father didn't give me those things. His roots might not have mattered to me if he, himself, had something to offer. But he didn't. And as the years went on and I grew older, he was increasingly absent.

Dad worked in a shipyard in Long Beach. It was a private enterprise, not the U.S. Navy. He may have worked there before the war. He did not go to college and never had the educational background that Mom did. He loved the ocean and took me deep-sea fishing several times. If there is a memory, fond or not, of being with my dad, it has to do with fishing, whether deep-sea or freshwater in the Sierra. In the course of my student ministry on a college campus in Missouri, I met a guy from Ohio who had never seen a mountain or a trout. I remember writing my dad after that just to thank him for the fact that I knew what a mountain was and what a trout was and had caught many.

***

Memories of my earliest years would include:

The loss of our dog, Perky, after she got out when a neighbor came over. Hit by a car. How long did I resent that neighbor? Or my parents for not going to find Perky before she was killed?

We picked up a stray cat that was emaciated. Slowly she grew and filled out. Then she had kittens. That first litter was a mess of dead and deformed babies that she would not care for, knowing that they were not healthy and would die. I can remember screaming at that "loveless" cat/momma.

I have a big birthmark on the outside of my right calf. I was ashamed of that for so long. When I crossed a street on foot, with a car stopped for me, and if I was wearing shorts, and I often was, I tried to hide my right leg from view. Pretty hard to do when you are walking. Most kids probably have memories like this. All I know is, I was so ashamed of it.

At school, when teams were chosen for softball, kickball, or whatever, I was one of those who got "delegated." "I had Farnsley last time. You guys take him." I never wanted the ball to come my way, as I was afraid I'd drop it or completely miss it.

Waiting for my dad to come home on Friday nights. If I had done my chores, like mowing the lawn, then I looked forward to his arrival, although I don't recall ever being complimented on my work. At least, unsolicited. I only remember when I did not do well.

That, in itself, was not worthy of a spanking, but there were plenty of other times that were. I remember being given the choice: hand or razor strop. The razor strop hung on the towel rack in our bathroom. It was a long strip of leather, maybe 3 or 4 inches wide. Dad would sharpen his straight razor on it. Which to choose? I chose the strop, as it didn't seem to hurt as his hand would. I did not have the attitude presented in the film, "Good Will Hunting," when he chose the wrench, with the attitude of "f--- you." I was just watching out for myself. Dad wasn't overly abusive, but I did get my share.

Later in my teen years, I remember overhearing my best friend's mom, whom I really liked, mention that my dad was an alcoholic. I yelled at her, "My dad is NOT an alcoholic," when all the time I knew he was. I knew how he passed out every night in his chair. I knew the night there was a police car in our driveway after following my father's erratic driving.

There were happy times as well – waking on a birthday morning and following the string attached to my bed until it led to a present somewhere.

Vacations to Wyoming or Lake Tahoe. Passing through Las Vegas and sending Mom out with $5 of my money to put into a slot machine.

Sometimes she came back with nothing. Sad. Sometimes with more than I gave her. Happy.

***

The ideas that we have about ourselves so often are formed in those early childhood years. I was a chunky kid. There was an even smaller kid in the neighborhood who would stand outside my house and call "Porky Pig." Over and over. "Porrrrrrrrrrrrky Pig . . . Porrrrrrrrrrrrky Pig." The other kids thought it was funny. But I thought I was a porky pig. When we played neighborhood football and, if we were to play tackle football, then I would be one of the first chosen. That was because if they gave me the ball, and I could get going, I was hard to bring down. On the other hand, if we played a flag or touch game, then I would be the last chosen, as I was so awkward and not real agile. One time, after I had scored or made a big play, one of the kids said it sure was great that I was so fat. I ran home crying.

I never could shake that image of me being fat. Even after I stretched out in my teens. Even when I was in great shape doing a lot of backpacking in later years. I still saw myself as fat. Couple that with this nagging SSA I had and my self-image was not great.

I did not think my dad was proud of me, or that I was the apple of his eye. I am big on those two phrases - your dad being proud of you and being the apple of his eye. I have read a lot about those topics. Many young and older men feel the same way. It is not a question of love, as many of us would say that our fathers did love us. It's that feeling that dad thinks I'm special. He is proud of me even though I have done nothing unusual to make him feel that way. That feeling of knowing you are the "apple of his eye." I can dismiss it, as my dad probably did not feel that either from his own father. It has been pointed out to me that this is not an excuse for him for not "being there" as a dad should. As I say elsewhere, it has become a great joy for me to be that reaffirming man to the younger bucks who come out to the deck for Deck Therapy. It's wonderful to know someone believes in you and says so.

***

As years went by, Dad had an increasing struggle with alcohol. He ended up in a 12-Step Program house for a period of time. I had never heard of that before, nor since. It was there for him when he needed drying out. He and Mom were divorced by then.

As I recall, and I could be wrong, all his brothers fought alcohol in one fashion or another. When I was about 10, I heard the story of another of my dad's brothers whom I never knew. I heard that this uncle, who lived in the Midwest, had gotten drunk one winter night, passed out in a snowbank, and froze to death. I could be mistaken because we never talked about it. But I have never forgotten that story and image. Another nail in the coffin I was building of poor family and self-image.

About the same time, I remember going out to our back yard and being mad and frustrated about the "Farnsley" name and the heritage I had. I thought it was a bad name, a cursed name, and I vowed that it needed to die, swearing that I would never have children because I did not want to pass on such a bad seed. I think it was one of the few vows I ever made that I really meant . . . at least at the moment. Some might say, "Aha! Here is where Rob went the SSA route." But, trust me, I was already dealing with that. Still, it didn't keep me from thinking that I would be married one day.

But "Farnsley" being a good name? Even today I struggle with that. My "little Robbie" still has negative thoughts about my name: shame, inadequate, dysfunctional.

***

In those years when I wanted less and less to be a Farnsley, the person I did want to be like was "Uncle Marvin" next door. He and his wife, "Aunt Margaret," had a cabin in the Sierra Nevada. Although they have long since passed away, their boys kept it and I still go there. I am like the fourth son. Uncle Marvin was an accountant. What I liked about him, and his job, was that he had money. When they bought a car, it was new. Their cabin in the Sierra was far better than the tent the Farnsleys camped in. They belonged to a country club, and I frequently went golfing with his sons, my closest friends at that time. It didn't matter that I didn't golf. I was the caddy. That was fun for me. Sometimes the boys would make bad shots, and they might throw their clubs in frustration. Far different from how I express anger. I am not sure that I ever had a way of expressing frustration or anger. I suppressed it. I was ever the peacemaker in our home. I just wanted things to be peaceful and calm. Thus, I never wanted to be, and am not, a violent or forceful person. I simply could not understand throwing a club. Anger issues aside, Uncle Marvin was able to provide all these luxuries, like cabins and golf club memberships.

His accounting office was not far away, and we could drop by there. It makes sense that I wanted to be an accountant through my years growing up. I was good with numbers and thought I could handle this and the good life and income it seemingly brought.

The shipyard, where my dad worked, was a far different place. I did get to go there a few times. It was in Long Beach and about a 30-minute drive away. The ships of varying sizes were cool. The dry dock where they worked on ships was also cool. But Dad's little cubicle of an office, and the rough pieces of tables and chairs, were not like Uncle Marvin's. Nor did I think there was a bottle of some kind of alcohol at Uncle Marvin's place as there was at Dad's office.

***

One safe haven for me is that cabin at Twin Lakes on the eastern side of the Sierra, not far from the Yosemite National Park boundary. I have been going there for more than 55 years. I invite friends to come for some of the time, and I have time alone there, as well. The cabin is the most "haunting" place in my life. In "The Sacred Romance" Curtis and Eldredge write about those places or events or smells in our youth that bring up memories or longings. They are "haunting" but not necessarily in a negative way. There is no place that has remained so consistent through most of my life. The smells, sounds, view, and memories. Thanks, Bob, Dick, and Steve (the owners....sons of Uncle Marvin). They don't even know my secret yet, but I have no fear that it will affect our friendship one bit.

***

My sister is about 2½ years older than me. In high school, she was pretty and popular, a Homecoming Princess, and smart. I think she was the salutatorian in her class. Not the top dog, but maybe second. We had the same algebra teacher. I remember her asking me, on report card day, why I wasn't as smart as my sister. The teacher was a fat, smelly woman with a Southern drawl. I was not so fast on my feet, or disrespectful, that I would have given a smart answer. But I wish I had.

I was Janet's little brother, and we fought like brothers and sisters might. I wanted to see everything she was doing with her friends, and I bugged her badly. When she left for college, our relationship changed. We became very close and remain that way. She does not see our family and her upbringing as I do. Although she knew as well that dad drank too much and was becoming alcoholic, I think she felt it was a relatively normal family and life. She was much more assertive than I in those days, and she and Dad had some good verbal fights when she knew she was right or disagreed about curfew times or something else. I just wanted to keep peace in the house. I can remember sitting at the empty dinner table, after everyone else has stormed away, wondering why we just can't have a peaceful dinner and conversation.

I know it is hard for my sister to read my perspective of some of these things. But one thing we agreed on, I think, was that Mom needed to leave Dad. The marriage needed to end. That did not happen until I was graduated from high school. Janet was already off at college, and getting ready to be married herself. But our parents waited until I was out of high school.

Even though I thought my parents should divorce, and Dad didn't really fight it, I remember how devastated Dad was when he read what Mom had written in the area of "incompatible differences." I don't know what she put in the divorce papers but, when Dad saw them, he wondered how she could say such things that were not true. Probably, there were words about affairs, alcohol, abuse and so on. She admitted that they were not true, but phrases and words like that were required for the court to grant the divorce. As I say, it devastated Dad.

***

When I came to Christ at 19, a bit of a complication arose. What does the Bible say about divorce? All of a sudden I found myself not so supportive of the idea, although I had thought for years that it needed to happen. Eventually I learned of a woman that he moved in with when he moved out of our house. They eventually married. Apparently, he had spent time with her, and she comforted him as he went through the separation. She took a gun from him when he first came. Which he was thinking of using on himself. Adultery then came into the mix, and I thought mom had more Biblical grounds. Not that she was looking for them. I was. When the divorce did happen and when Dad was out of the house, it was a peaceful time. There hadn't been a lot of arguing; it was just a matter of tension. I don't like tension.

Mom took a renewed interest in cooking wonderful Sunday lunches. I remember having lobster and frog legs. Something we never had growing up, but now she wanted to cook for me and Linda, my sister's best friend, who was living with us.

Linda is still like a sister to me. She went to a local college and needed a place to stay. She roomed with us and was there during my parents' separation. To this day, I am thankful for her and her husband, Steve. Their home is like a hacienda on 20 acres or so, and it became a refuge for me after my world crashed and I was at the counseling center in California. I love going there. I feel so loved and accepted. My sister's place is equally like that. Safe. Protected. Full of unconditional love. I wonder whether you have safe places like these. I never knew how much I needed them until my world did crash.

***

Although I never feared for my physical well-being at home (other than the razor strop), I don't think I felt totally safe. I certainly did not feel safe to bring up the SSA issue, which I was slowly seeing ever more clearly in myself. Had I shared that with Mom and Dad, their responses would have been more in the area of denial. "You do not! Look at you! You are a good, growing boy!"

It was like when I was 6 and in the first grade. I tried to convince them that I could not hear out of my left ear. It had taken years for me to realize that this was not normal. Normal people actually DO hear out of both ears.

They would not accept it for a while, as I developed normally and I could hear them fine. It took some talking, but I was finally taken to an audiologist for tests, and, lo and behold, I was totally deaf in my left ear. I don't recall that I ever heard the definitive reason for this. There was some conjecture about a bad earache I had when quite young. In later years, I have learned that I don't have a fully developed ear drum. Thankfully, I had better-than-average hearing in my right. This discovery led to a year of trauma for me. In the second grade, it was decided that I should go to a special school with an aural education department. This was a precaution, in fear that I might lose my hearing in my good ear. I had to ride in a taxi with profoundly deaf kids. I was in a regular second grade class, but had to leave every day and go over with the deaf kids to try to learn to lip-read.

I hated those taxi rides. I hated those kids. I did not want to be like them or be rejected by others because I came with the deaf kids each day. I never did learn to lip-read, and was allowed to return to my neighborhood school for the second half of the year. I have often wondered over the years how my experience with the deaf kids has affected me. Did I feel like I really was like them? Did I feel like I had been dealt one more bad card in my already worsening hand of cards? Did I feel rejected and misunderstood? There is probably a bit of a "yes" in the answers.

***

Another childhood memory, around age 10 or maybe 12, was a visit to old family friends on vacation. Their son, a few years older than I, took me out back one day and proposed a "blow-job" experience. I had never heard of such a thing and quickly ran back inside. The whole idea turned me off and was one more unattractive sexual image. Post-crash, I have had several men tell me of their homosexual wanderings at an early age, although they are "hetero." It seems rather common that boys do some touching and other experimenting together. But not me. I never had "the talk" with my dad either, which might have helped at least a little. I was on my own to figure these things out, and I didn't seem to be going about it in the normal way, whatever that was.

Instead of "the talk," I have memories and images. The recurring image of my naked father flopped out (passed out from alcohol) on the bed on a hot night. I had to go by their bedroom to get to the bathroom and the door would frequently be open. There he would be in all his radiant glory, on his back, fully exposed. As I grew up, I saw that picture often. No wonder Mom went to sleep every night out in the living room in front of the TV. Who would want to go back to that? At least that is what I thought. I can't remember ever seeing them go to bed together.

Because we never had the talk, we never discussed things like masturbation. It was a topic that was not discussed by anyone after I came to Christ. It seems like Christians of my era just didn't want to know. Or ask. Which now makes it so amazing to me with the young bucks who come to the deck. The topic is not taboo at all. Yet it is an area of much frustration to guys. It seems it is today's litmus test of spirituality that young men put on themselves.

***

Another of my fondest childhood memories was going to the Merced area in Central California. Our family's closest friends lived there and eventually moved to a nine-acre farm in the country. They had cows, chickens, gardens, and a horse. Had anything ever happened to my parents in my childhood, I would have gone to live with Floyd and Aletha Schelby and their son, Mark.

Aletha was living in our home the day I was born in 1945. Floyd was at sea, in the Navy. So I have known her since Day One. When my mom died (a year after Dad), I found myself asking Aletha and Floyd whether I might call them Mom and Dad. They had no problem with that. They were Mom and Pop to me for years.

Aletha would take Mark and me to swim in the ice-cold irrigation canal that was not far off. Sometimes we went skinny-dipping by moonlight. We four would play Rummy (a card game) at night for an hour or two. Mark and I against his mom and dad. The winners, over the weeks I was there, were taken into town for ice cream. Looking back, why did Mark and I always win? They seemed to me like an "intact" family where love was expressed, especially by Aletha. I often wished I lived with them. In later years, Aletha was always a supportive, non-judgmental person. As I said, I called them Mom and Pop. Mark is my "bro." Their place is another safe haven for me. I have been, and am, loved and accepted. I am a thankful man.

Why do I discuss all these events? I suppose to try to explain a bit why I retreated further and further into my own self and mind. It seemed to be the only safe place I could go with my secret. I mentioned various safe places in previous paragraphs. But I only became aware of them, and their safety, after my secret came out. I never would have admitted it before. And my secret? It got stuffed in there with all the rest of the things I thought I could not discuss.

Chapter Three

Being a Big Brother

"He ain't heavy, Father, he's my brother." — *Boys Town slogan*

As I reached my early 30s, I had seemingly turned a healthy corner from all those negative childhood experiences. I started teaching elementary school, fifth and sixth grades combined. The school was on the west side of Fresno, so was mostly made up of Hispanics and African-Americans. In the course of time, I had a favorite kid. That was Steve. He wasn't a great student, just a good kid, who did not have a dad. I took him, and others, to Fresno State basketball games and outings like that.

After Steve finished his sixth-grade year, he moved on to junior high and high school. We lost touch. Then, I started to see his name in the sports section of the local newspaper. He had grown a lot and was becoming a standout high school basketball player. I looked him up, and we reconnected. I could see that he was going to have a chance at a basketball scholarship when he finished high school. However, I was concerned about his grades. So I moved into his life once again and started trying to help him with his studies. I also exposed him to things he would have never known or done. We hiked to the top of Half Dome in Yosemite. I took him water skiing. He was funny to watch, trying to get that big body of his out of the water. He went with me to Lake Tahoe, where I went every summer. I taught him how to drive a stick shift. I was with him when he first tried to shave.

I became very attached to Steve. Extremely so. He fulfilled, at that time, the need I had (and still do) to love someone. Then the day came when we left Fresno for Las Cruces, New Mexico, where he had won a scholarship to play for New Mexico State University. We stopped by the Grand Canyon on the way. I had allocated about four days to be with him at his new school. He was a bit insecure and not sure about going away to college in a strange place. It was a big school, and unfamiliar surroundings and people. He quickly bonded with his new basketball buddies, and I could see that I was no longer needed. So I left a day or two early. I took him to dinner that last night and, when he left my car in the dorm parking lot and went on in, I sat there and bawled. I thought, "How do real parents deal with this? I am a basket case." A big hole was created in my life and my time.

I don't want to leave my Father out of this. God was very present in my life during all this. He was most important. I thanked Him daily for this relationship, and others. I talked with Steve often about his own relationship with Christ. I was very busy in discipleship at my church. My walk with God was consistent. Along with all that, however, I did have this great joy of walking with Steve.

My SSA was not an issue here at all. I had a need to love and be loved. To be needed by someone. To give myself to someone. I still do.

I returned to Fresno determined to find another "little brother" like Steve. Although I did not want to go through an organization (like Big Brothers[3]), fearing that if my secret were to be found out, I was sure to be disqualified. Not to mention the bureaucracy and other legal hassles those big organizations seem to have these days. I was thinking I would find someone in junior high. Instead, through a referral from a friend who knew I was looking, I found Justin, who was just 5. He had a single mom. I met with her, shared my journey with Steve, and why I was looking for someone else now that Steve was gone. We agreed to have me meet Justin on an afternoon. I think we went to McDonalds. Then, in a short time, we agreed for me to come get him and bring him over to my house for the night. Over the next five years, he, like Steve, worked his way into my heart. I went to his school for good and bad issues that came up. I visited his teachers, had him overnight almost every weekend, gave him baths, took him to McDonald's, disciplined him, and everything else a dad might do. Or a big brother. His mom would bring him over for discipline. When he was 10, and I left on my missionary journey, he was devastated, and so was I. I had arranged for a

---

3. The official name is Big Brothers Big Sisters of America.

good friend to take over as "big brother," but that bond did not happen instantly. I can still picture them driving away, as Justin slobbered all over himself through his tears.

Of the two, I remain in closer touch with Steve, although a year and more can go by before he may call me from England, where he lives. When we do connect, it is just like old times and he is so faithful to thank me for my investment in him. He wonders where he would be if I had not been there for him.

These were the first young people that I got involved with in a serious way, although not in a formal Christian way of mentoring. They certainly did fulfill a need I had to love and be loved – and still need – despite what some would wonder about it being "healthy." It was not a predatory thing. I am not sure that it was even altruistic, although I thought my involvement would be a good thing in their lives. It simply brought me joy and fulfillment.

At that time, I was probably less empathetic to female friends who were in their 30s and still single. The biological "time bomb" was ticking for them, and they didn't see any children in their future. I would suggest they do what I was doing. There are many fatherless or motherless kids out there, so go and "be there" for them. To any woman who is reading this, forgive me if I bluntly told you that.

These examples are other glimpses into my life and how I found, and still find, so much fulfillment by investing in others. The older I get, I find I cannot give too much affirmation, encouragement,and reminders of how proud I am of the men I work with. We all need that, as most of us, especially me, most likely did not get that kind of loving affirmation from our fathers.

I will say again that, in these current times , if I were to go to Big Brothers or a similar organization, I believe I would not be accepted because of my same-sex attraction. I can understand why every group needs to be careful, but it seems that SSA is an automatic disqualifier where being "hetero" is not. I don't think I could get a volunteer position in most churches for child care, much less a paid position.

In my view, SSA is like being heterosexual, except that your object of interest is of the same sex. Generally, the physical struggles would be the same. One would move into homosexual or heterosexual relationships. But many in both camps remain celibate. That may be for different reasons which I won't go into here. I do think that if one applies for a job and says they are hetero, but celibate, that will not be an issue. But if one admits to being homosexual in their outlook, but remains celibate, that person will be looked upon at least somewhat more unfavorably. That may not be reality, but it is my perception, and thus my reality.

Something for which I am thankful in all this is that my SSA has not interfered with me in my journey in men's ministry. Men's ministry was a safe place for me to be involved with men, and yet not have the question one gets after two or three dates with a woman: "Well, what's up? Are you two getting serious?" With guys, that question never comes up. People aren't wondering how serious the relationship is getting. They are just glad that I was there for them, guys who needed the Lord or needed to grow spiritually. On the other hand, as I got older, people would want to know: "Why are you not married?" Although that question bothered me, it was a normal question to ask. Thankfully, they were not wondering whether anything "weird" was going on in my discipling times with men. There wasn't anything weird going on. I have been asked if these times were a temptation for me. They were not. I longed for relationships with people. Beyond that there was nothing. I loved the men that I felt God had entrusted to me. It is as simple as that.

Chapter Four

My Christian Journey

"Perhaps the supreme achievement of the Holy Spirit in the life of ragamuffins is the miraculous movement from self-rejection to self-acceptance." — Brennan Manning, *The Ragamuffin Gospel*

How did I get to a place where I was deemed by myself and others to be equipped to disciple people? I certainly did not go to a Bible college and take courses in it. Here's some background.

I grew up in a Lutheran church. My mother and grandmother would take me. My dad rarely went, although he held various church offices over the years. The church was a couple of blocks down the street from our house. I could walk there. I was a "good boy." I was an acolyte. Those are the young boys who follow the priest or pastor around the altar area. Another term for that would be "altar boy." I was confirmed around age 13. That meant I could take communion. I was groomed by the pastor to be a pastor myself. At least that was his hope, I think. As someone who always wanted to help others, I wasn't opposed. As I grew older, I began to have doubts, and was not sure whether I believed in God at all. Nevertheless, I would still kneel by my bed and pray to an unknown God that, if I could be of help to others, I would pursue this.

During high school, I still attended church, although I was growing more and more distant from God and doubting my faith. No one would have suspected anything of the sort. I made periodic visits to such groups as Youth for Christ, but they really held no interest for me, nor did the youths who went to those meetings. In fact, I didn't even want to be identified with them.

***

This change was a part of my total transformation of identity during high school. I wanted to escape my old crowd and become one of "the boys." They were the guys who wore white T-shirts, Levi's, and went out drinking on weekends. Think of movie idol James Dean, if you are not too young to know who he was – the ultimate "Rebel Without a Cause," one of his most celebrated films. My reputation? Friends knew I could drink beer and a lot of it. Had I not come to Christ in a more significant way, I truly believe I would be dead today, adding to the evidence that alcoholism ran in my family.

After my senior year of high school, I went with some friends to Disneyland for the evening. We picked up some liquor and tried to sneak it in with us. Two of us got caught. I remember being led across a back lot, trying to quietly lay down the flask of whiskey. I was not real steady, and it rattled. The officer heard it, turned around, and confiscated it. I told my friend to shut up and let me do the talking. Then, I fabricated a story about how we had been approached by someone on the way in, selling the stuff, so we bought it. The truth was, we bought it from someone before we ever left for the park. They separated me from my friend. When he came back, he was in tears. When I asked him what he said, he replied, "The truth." Well, my goose was cooked. Our parents were called, and they came and got us.

I got a lenient lecture on the way home. I don't remember whether I was punished, even in some minor way. Decades later I read John Eldredge, and he described how he was "missed" by his parents as a youth (he had broken into a house). His parents were there, physically present. But they didn't seem to care enough to deal with a very serious issue. In effect, they missed the opportunity to engage their son and "see" him. He wanted to be seen. I thought about my drinking and my run-in with the law. Not wanting to be punished, I am sure I was very happy at the time. Looking back, I wonder how "missed" I felt. My parents weren't even concerned enough to make me pay in a severe way for drinking, lying, and breaking the law. I think I wanted them to see me, and they didn't. A similar experience would be the first time I got drunk. I came home, mom was in her chair late at night, as usual. I went to bed and later threw up in the bathroom. In a stupor, I walked out and woke mom up to tell her I had thrown up and she said to go to bed and she would take care of it. The next day she commented that my vomit reeked of alcohol, which must have come from the portion of the "highball" (mixed drink) that my dad was having and from which I had several sips. Mix that with the take-out hamburgers we had, and that must have caused it. I, of course, agreed. Amazed that my mom could be so naive. That is being missed. Maybe intentionally to save me, and possibly her, from embarrassment.

***

When I was graduated from high school, I applied to several colleges. I finally was accepted to the University of California at Berkeley. It was too late, however, to get a room in the dorms. The only other living situation, besides an apartment, was a Greek social fraternity. I signed up to "rush" a fraternity. All the literature suggested to narrow the choices down to just a few before rush, as there was little time for someone to cement relationships before bids went out.

I went up to Berkeley for the rush weekend in August. I checked into a hotel near campus and then set off to various engagements at the fraternity houses I wanted to pursue. As much as the literature might have said how important grades were to a fraternity, or having men who were involved in school government, areas where I thought I might be an asset, all they really wanted were "jocks" – quarterbacks or wide receivers, or football, baseball or basketball lettermen. I was not that.

After an intense, drunken weekend, I could see that I would not receive a bid. I was relegated to the side rooms at the parties. I was quite embittered at what I perceived as the hypocrisy of the fraternities and their literature. I didn't need that. I called my mom to say I was coming home. I could sign up for a dorm room in the spring semester and in the meantime go to Compton Junior College. She didn't want that. She told me to stay in Berkeley while she did some phoning around to see whether she might come up with someone who would let me board with them. After about a day, I said, "Enough." I was heading for home. The issue really was, with me out of the house, Mom could more readily leave Dad. My coming back complicated things. On my way to Southern California, I stopped by Merced where the Schelbys, our close family friends, lived. Aletha,

Mom's close friend, affirmed my decision and cheered me on. Aletha did not agree with Mom. So I continued on home and enrolled in Compton Junior College.

**

At age 19, while attending Compton JC, I had a falling out with my closest high school friend, and was on the hunt for new friends. I was invited to an InterVarsity Christian Fellowship meeting. To my surprise, I kind of liked it – never mind that some who went were the same boring people I had rejected in high school. I continued to go and started attending the same church as some of those InterVarsity people.

About six months later, I realized that I had never made a personal decision for Jesus. If you're raised in the church as I was, it simply is what you do and supposedly believe. I was an American. I was baptized. I was confirmed in the Lutheran church. I loved apple pie. I even sort of believed in God. What else could I be but a Christian? But I saw that I was not a "Christian" as these new friends were. They definitely had something more personal and real than I. So, I resolved that issue in May of 1965 and made my decision for Christ. That led to a high involvement in Christian groups and studies. The Bible took on new meaning for me. I never knew it could be relevant in my life. I had this new, intimate, at least for me, relationship with God. People actually desired to be with me. They thought I had something to offer. It was all so new and exciting to me, and I had acquired some good friends.

**

I learned the concepts that good Christians don't drink, go to movies, dance, play cards, or smoke. I did them all, but gladly gave them up. I changed churches, feeling that my old church had totally misled me – tricking me into thinking I was a Christian when, in fact, I was not. Certainly, the pastor was simply teaching me the Lutheran way. It was not as if he knew he was living a lie and was trying to deceive me and others into following the same way. He and my parents thought I had gotten sucked into some kind of cult. For my part, I thought they were all unbelievers at that church.

Time has mellowed me. I am not really concerned anymore as to when I was "saved." Maybe I was in all those early years. I am only concerned now that I, or anyone else, walk with Jesus, and know His saving grace and love.

During this time, my first summer of being a Christian, I did something that really disappointed and embarrassed my dad, and further cemented in his mind that I was being controlled by a cult. Through his work at the shipyard, Dad had come across a man with a large yacht. That summer this man was going to take it from Long Beach, through the Panama Canal and up to New York. Dad had gotten him to agree to take me on as a deckhand for the trip. I admit it was a most amazing summer prospect. But I was a new believer, growing in my faith. After consulting with my new pastor and his son, my best friend then, I decided that this would not be a good thing for me to do at the time. It would remove me from this nurturing environment in which I was growing so much in my newfound faith. It would put me into a carnal world of seamen that would not be good for me. My dad was furious. He argued. He yelled. He probably raised his hand as if to hit me. It convinced him more than ever that I was under the control of a cult. I am sure he had gone out on a limb to get me this chance and thought I would jump at it. When I did not, he was humiliated to have to go back to the yacht owner and tell him I would not be aboard.

***

My decision for Christ caused me to make many other decisions that took me in different directions from what I had planned. First, I had planned to return to Cal. That had already changed when I changed my major to forestry. Next, I was headed to Humboldt State, in Arcata, in extreme northern California, and a dorm room. I could see now that this was not the answer for me either. I wanted to stay right where I was, continue to grow in my faith, and serve our InterVarsity Club at Compton JC. So I stayed there for a second year.

I don't regret those decisions. I think they were good. However, as I do reflect on it all, I was heavily influenced by those I respected. I had become a key part of the group; they did not want to lose me. I would play that same role for others today. I want to mentor young men into believing they have what it takes and following their hearts. I was learning from these early examples in my life.

***

I moved on to a four-year college, Long Beach State. I remained very involved in InterVarsity, as well as my church's college group. Another life-changing experience was the training that Campus Crusade for Christ (now known as Cru) did in those days. Because our church was centrally located in Los Angeles, Crusade wanted to do the week-long training at the church. I was aware of Crusade's style of "aggressive evangelism" and was not so sure I would attend. At the same time, my style of "friendship evangelism" had led to no conversations about Christ, and certainly no one professed faith in Him with me. I decided this might be good for me.

During the week, we had "front-line training" at the beach, where we would take surveys and follow up with a presentation of the "Four Spiritual Laws." The first day, nothing happened, no one responded, and I got sunburned. Thanks a lot, God. I was very leery the second day we went out. The first guy we met had a broken leg in a cast and was sunning himself. He was not very mobile. He agreed to take the survey and then listen to the "Four Spiritual Laws." I shared the four laws with him, and he prayed to receive Christ!

It was an amazing experience for me, something I had never done. Plus, he was so thankful that we would come down and share this with him. Well, I was the thankful one. We have long since lost touch, and I know nothing about his life since then, but I know his name was Dick L. I won't spell his last name, but I remember it 48 years later. That training was key in my Christian journey, and I am thankful to say that I have had many similar experiences since the one with Dick. It started the development of my ability to relate with people and talk with them about Jesus.

***

Toward the end of my time at college, I met a guy named Greg, who had just come to Christ. We became friends, and I was a mentor to him. I dislike saying "discipled," because I don't think it was that focused. We did spend much time looking at Scriptures and dealing with his questions. He certainly looks to me as the one who began the discipleship journey for him. It might have gone on, but I moved away to my new work at the University of Missouri with Campus Crusade for Christ, which I had joined as a campus staff member. I recently had a phone conversation with him, which we do about every six weeks.

Greg reminded me of his fraternity brother, who came to Christ due to his influence. Greg discipled him before they moved on after they were graduated the following year. This man has gone on to become the president of a significant missionary organization.

Over his life, he has had a significant impact on a major portion of the world for the cause of Christ. He will soon be retiring and returning to the country where he first started his missionary journey. This guy is in my "downline,"[4] partly due to the investment I made in Greg's life. We never know what will become of the lives we touch and reach out to.

My college life had been focused on graduating. Even that was a less-than-satisfying experience. My family, except for my dad, had moved away. When I took my last final exam, I walked down the hall, out to the car, and drove away. My degree was mailed to me. There were no parties, no graduation ceremony, no congratulatory cards, nothing. It just ended and I moved on. A rite of passage missed.

***

One of the first people I led to Christ in my new campus ministry in Missouri took a long time to make that decision. We had many meetings and lots of discussions. Some of my colleagues kidded me about the time I was wasting as this guy obviously was never going to make that decision. But he did make it. He has gone on to be a highly popular college professor and writer of several deep-thinking Christian books. He has had a huge impact on many people. We never know.

***

Over the years, I dated some of the ladies in the various Christian groups I was involved with. The same problem always arose. When it seemed an appropriate time for holding hands, or a goodnight kiss, I was not interested.

***

My 4½ years with Campus Crusade for Christ in Missouri were excellent years for me. My knowledge of ministry grew – sharing my faith, discipling, talking with guys – and they were productive years in terms of professions of faith. To this day, I think that whatever skills or abilities I may have in these areas, they were honed on the campuses of Missouri. I am forever grateful.

I was reminded the other day, as I was listening to an old song by Simon and Garfunkel, "The Boxer," of the days in the Student Union at the university and the numerous times I was sitting with some

---

4. "Downline" comes from pyramid businesses where the people you recruit to work under you are your "downline."

student, who was praying to receive Christ, while that song was on the juke box. Along with "Hey Jude," by the Beatles. Those were long songs, and many people considered Christ while they were playing.

But in those years, did anyone know of my secret? No. I am not sure I had yet admitted it to myself. I knew I had an attraction, but I still somehow thought I would work through it.

***

From Missouri, I returned to California and took a job at a small, privately owned, Christian camp called Emerald Cove Camp. It's located at Bass Lake in the Sierra foothills, not far from Yosemite National Park. It was owned then by the Jim Slevcove family. They have been wonderful friends to me.

My job was to set up and lead a backpacking program for youth groups. The camp provided the equipment, food, and guide. Youth leaders brought approximately 10 kids with a few adults and away we would go for a week on High Sierra trails. I would lead them to a lake and stay with them for the week. I was not responsible for programming, so I had lots of time to fish, hike, read, daydream. I was in the best physical shape of my life in those days. I could carry two backpacks up the mountainside. I was no "Porky Pig," although I still saw myself as fat.

***

Before I started at the camp, I was "Bob." My name is Robert, and I was called "Robbie" as a child and that became "Bob" as I got older. Sometimes, as a kid, I was called "Red" because of my reddish complexion. I hated that nickname. I did not like that I was fair-skinned, reddish, and freckled, and always susceptible to sunburn. It was during that time of working at the camp that my name changed from "Bob" to "Rob." Jim, the owner, had a habit of taking guys' names and putting a "y" or "ie" on the end. He started calling me "Robbie." That got shortened to Rob and I liked it. I felt like "rugged Rob."

I was splitting firewood, doing all kinds of woodsy things, as well as cooking, cleaning, and various other chores during the winter months when churches came to use our facilities for weekend retreats. During the weeks in the winter, we would go skiing for a day after a storm had blown through. It was during these three-plus years that I first saw myself as "manly." I was about 29.

When the summers ended, I went backpacking alone for a week at a time. Although I loved doing that, it was also a time when, as I watched a glorious sunset and alpenglow, I wished I had a partner to share it with.

***

Manly. What does that mean? Guys probably all have their ideas and wishes of accomplishing "manhood." Surely, it is more than just going through puberty and being able to father children. Even with that simple definition, I don't think I have ever felt like a man because I do not think I could perform accordingly to make it happen. So I have had that big arrow in my chest all my life, along with all the other things I thought I could not do athletically, mechanically (like repair things), attitudinally, even spiritually.

In these last eight years, I have finally come to embrace my "beloved son-ness." I believe that my Heavenly Father is quite proud and fond of me just the way I am. Even with SSA. But, as usual, I can still doubt. Recently, one of the young bucks who is a regular on the deck and knows my story said something like this: "Rob, when conversations go to being a man or knowing a man, the first person I think of is you." Me!? SSA me!? Comments like that, from real flesh-and-blood people, are so courage-giving. This guy believes in me. Oh, that I would have heard it from my dad!

***

Despite all that I've said against my name, one fond memory while working at the camp includes the naming of "Farnsley Peak." You won't find that name on any U.S. Forest Service map, but I know where it is. Just across the ridge line from Madera Peak is another outcropping of boulders. You can scramble up the boulders to the top. Once there, you see a straight drop down the other side toward Lady Lake. From Lady Lake, you look up a very impressive massif to Farns Peak at the top.

Are you interested in finding it? Take Beasore Road from Bass Lake. Pass a granite outcropping that rock climbers like to climb, called, seriously, "The Balls." You will find them identified on maps. Then take the trail to Jackass Lakes, and Farns Peak is above the highest of the three lakes (Upper Jackass). Good names to be associated with!

One summer, a group of us put a register there. A can with a tablet and pencil in it so people could "sign in" once getting to the top, assuming they knew where to look in the rocks to find the can. The following summer I went up with some people, but the can was gone. So, only the "in people" know about Farns Peak and where it is located. I would not mind having my ashes scattered from there at the end of my days.

Another fond memory is the creation of Farns Bars, or Mountain Bars. I took a granola recipe that my mom had and made big batches on a weekend. Then, that was put into a batter and baked, and it made a very nutritious granola bar of sorts. We would provide Farns Bars for a few of the lunches each week.

"Farns" was used a lot in reference to me because somewhere in that time frame, the TV show "Happy Days" was popular. Henry Winkler played the character of "the Fonz." Fonz and Farns are beloved terms. "Farns" is not "Farnsley," and I still did not care for that name. But as time went by, and goes by, my friends have all changed. No one knows of my childhood. I have probably grown more comfortable with my name over the years.

***

I learned some good lessons at that camp. There were times when, as I might be vacuuming a dorm, I would wonder what happened to me? I had been in this highly interactive and productive ministry and now I am vacuuming floors. I prayed a lot as I worked, but still . . . . Then I read Psalm 1. It talks about the man whose delight is in the law of the Lord. He is like a tree planted by streams of water, which YIELDS ITS FRUIT IN SEASON. The concept of seasons entered my life.

Sometimes we are dormant, sometimes we're leafing out, and sometimes we bear fruit. Over my life I have had more than one of each of those seasons. I am thankful for the productive times, for when a person is dormant he tends to wonder what he is good for. Then I remember. Productive seasons don't always mean leading people to Christ. I think I am quite productive these days, and I am not doing much evangelistically. At any rate, my life at that camp was "dormant" to the observer, and to me. But the roots continued to go deeper.

A recurring image from those backpacking years is seeing fallen trees in various stages of decomposition. If you look closely, you usually will see new trees starting to grow out of the fallen, rotted one. New life coming from old. Almost as if new life cannot come unless old life dies. Many of us have already realized that, or pay lip service to it, but that image is very clear in helping one understand the truth of it.

It always was an irritation to me when I would realize I had hiked the last section of trail with my head almost always looking down. Rarely did I look up. I wondered what I had missed by not looking up more frequently. Maybe a mountain lion had been up on a high rock or some other animal moving through the forest. To me, the lesson was that I am too concerned with little, mundane things and don't think much about what God is doing. I am looking down on my own issues and not looking at the bigger picture of what God is up to.

***

Another lesson. One of my new friends I had made at the camp, Dave, was with me one day. He was sharing some of his "stuff" and wondering what to do about it. But not in a way that he was asking for help or advice. I was thinking, "Don't you know who I am? I was a campus minister, of sorts, for years. People came to me with their 'stuff' just because of my position and not because they knew a thing about me or my walk with God. I was simply a 'staff guy' and therefore qualified to help them."

But he was not asking me. He was simply sharing with his Christian brother, and I realized that I had to earn the right to be asked for opinions and advice. I listened – a very good skill to have – and over time earned that right from him and others. It is so easy, in our Christian subculture, to think that because someone has been to seminary, for example, he or she is qualified to speak "truth" into us. And we, without questioning, accept it. After all, this person has studied the Bible for years and has a Master's of Divinity degree. I struggle with that all the time. Until these later years in my life, I was always willing to defer to someone else's opinion because they had more education. Not anymore.

***

Another arrow in my self-image was inflicted at the camp, however. After my first summer, I was in great shape. Not fat. Because I have a reddish complexion, I have had to be careful about sunburns my whole life. That first summer, I slowly exposed myself to the sun and became adjusted to it. I went without a shirt most of the time. At 9,000 feet. My beige "tan" was the best I'd ever had.

That fall, I noticed a mole that I'd had on my stomach all my life. It seemed to be changing a bit. It turned out to be melanoma. The deadliest type of skin cancer. I'd never heard of it before, so was not real nervous about it. The operation to remove it left a scar about the size of a softball on my abdomen. That eliminated the "no-shirt" lifestyle for me. With the scar, I rarely went swimming or to the beach, as I did not want to take off my shirt and be stared at all the time. It was my issue. Probably not the big deal that I made it out to be, but with the self-image I had anyway, it was a big deal.

***

After 3½ years at the camp, I prepared to move on. My secret? No one knew. I was getting more and more hints that I should be finding a life partner. But that was more difficult than anyone knew, and besides, I was living a full and productive life. I was happy.

My plan was to move to Fresno and go back to college and earn a teaching credential. That would give me free summers to hike, I thought. Before returning to college, I set aside six months to hike the Pacific Crest Trail with my friend, Alan.

We started at the Mexican border in the spring and planned to hike the entire trail, ending at the Canadian border in the fall, before deep, heavy snows fell. We lasted a month. It was a great experience, but so much of the trail was temporary in those days, and we found ourselves walking along a lot of highways because the trail rights had not been acquired.[5] We walked 22 miles a day with no let up, if you're going to make Canada – 2,663 miles away – by the fall. After that month of walking so many roadsides and temporary trails, we decided that we didn't need to be the "first" to do the trail in some bizarre way – first to do the trail south to north, north to south, first to do it alone, first to do it pregnant. There seemed to be a lot of egos out there, and we wanted to enjoy life a bit more. We had no agenda to be the "first" in some way to do the trail. I can't even say "because it was there," as someone did. We just wanted to try and do it. I kept a journal and recorded diligently why we came to our decision so that, when I might look back remorsefully, I would know why we decided

5. The PCT, as it is commonly known, was designated a National Scenic Trail in 1968. It was officially completed in 1993.

what we did. I returned to Fresno and did sections of the trail that summer, when they were intended to be hiked. I never did complete the trail. Writing that last sentence does cause some pangs of remorse or regret. Am I a quitter? I don't think so. We tried to do something that never was intended to be done in one fell swoop. Now, I better understand why. Some parts are better in the spring. Others in the fall. Few of them in the winter. You can't do that if you are going from border to border as fast as you can.

***

I spent a year getting my elementary teaching credential, and then got a job in the Fresno Unified School District. You know for sure that, as I applied for the job, I didn't tell my secret. Thankfully, there were no such probing questions on the application. If my secret had come out, I would be labeled, automatically, a child abuser or some worse perversion. What else could a homosexual be?

In those years, I got very involved in my church – choir, singles group, men's ministry. I consider that I was very effective, and appreciated.

In our church setup, we only had deacons. No elders. We handled many church issues. At the time, I was asked to be on the board, and a good friend, who was on the church staff, encouraged me to accept the position. His thinking was that a single man could represent all the "disenfranchised" groups at church . . . singles, women (women were NOT on the board), divorced people. Little did he know what other group I might have represented. But I don't think that would have mattered to him. At any rate, I did accept and did serve. For one year, I was chairman of that board.

***

In those years, I was also jokingly known as running a "halfway" house for men in transition. I had, at different times, some good brothers whose wives left them. The men needed a place to stay and maybe a good brother. I took them in. One of my reasons for doing so was self-centered. I could see that the longer I lived alone, the more set in my ways I became. I was hopeful that some of my sharp edges might be a bit rounded off.

When I saw the heartache these guys went through, I thought that maybe I was lonely at times, but at least I wasn't going to go through what they were, when someone you love leaves you. I also could see my own heart and how I could do the same thing if I were married. I could easily end up saying, "This is painful, I am sorry I am doing it, but I am leaving you. Life is too short to live like this the rest of my days. You'll get over it." I could do that. I thought, "It is better for me to just stay to myself."

But again, I could not let on who I really was. Why? The same reasons. I feared I would be rejected. I would be put out of the church. I was a Realtor-associate and did not fear for my job, but so much of that job comes from your contacts, and most of mine came from Christian sources.

***

Before departing on my missionary journey in 1991, I had been a Realtor for 11 years. Those were the days of high interest rates, and the housing boom in California and the Central Valley had gone bust.

Back in 1980, when I entered the business, I had a friend, who had been doing very well. I figured I would like to enjoy the material lifestyle that I saw in him. Had I been married in those early days, I would have never made it. I took a part-time job and borrowed money from good friends to make ends meet. I had purchased a house early on, and it looked like I would lose it. But a thought I have had so often through life is: "It's only me. So what if I lose the house? I can move in with friends. I will get by some way. Thankfully I am not married with two kids. If I were, I don't know what I would do." This does not sound as if it is dependent on God. I do think His presence was in my thinking, but my thinking was pretty much of needing to take care of myself. When all else fails, I will turn to Him. Having said that, my Christian life was all-important to me.

***

Those years as a Realtor were, overall, great years. I worked as little as I could so that I might do the things that were really important to me. A client of mine, a financial planner, had come by my house and saw my cozy place. He asked, "When are you going to move up?" After all, I was in real estate. My reply was something like: "Why would I want to do that? This place is fine for me. I don't need bigger bills. I want a low overhead so that I might do the things that are important to me, which do not include working more than I do." What was important to me? Discipling men one on one.

I remember walking down the street one day, reflecting on where I was in life. My cozy house was a perfect place for me. I had a job that I enjoyed. I was discipling 10 men individually. I thought, "Lord, if I can come to the end of my life and see that I have invested in 10 men who are now walking with you, what more could I ask? That would be a life well-lived." Thankfully, there are far more than 10 now. They are scattered all over the world.

Thoughts of my secret, SSA, rarely entered my mind. That was my secret and God's, and it was safely tucked away, never to be found. I think I had lived with it so long, and found ways to live a fulfilling life, I gave up praying that God would take it away. I just accepted it and moved ahead.

***

One of the fun things I did in 1986 was to have a "Timothy Retreat." The "Operation Timothy" program was a series of Navigator books, about the first three in the overall series. The Christian Business Men's Committee had packaged them in their own efforts to disciple men who came to Christ through their work. Just as the Apostle Paul discipled a younger new believer, Timothy, the program was designed to do the same. Our church also adopted the package, as we had several men involved in CBMC.

I was never taken through "Timothy." I skipped that part and started taking other guys through. Over the years, we joked that God Himself took me through Timothy. When my Timothy completed the course, he in turn would take some other man through it, and I as well would find another man. Thus, we were building chains. The chains broke down over time, but some men were very faithful to take others, who took others. And I did the same.

So I decided to have a Timothy Retreat to see how the chains extending from me were going. I invited about 30 men. I brought in the man who brought me to Christ, Ed, as the speaker. It was quite moving and a challenge to all to see how you can make an impact by doing Timothy. It was real joy to Ed to see how God had used me. It turned into a great weekend.

***

As you have read, I had a good campus ministry and a successful discipleship ministry at my home church. You could say I was "called" to each of them. I used that word early in my post-college career. In more recent years, I struggle with the use of the "C" word. . . "called." I like simply serving the Lord where I think I can help. It seems to me that even the Apostle Paul, when "called" to Macedonia, was already on his missionary journey. He went where God led him, as I hope I have, first in Indonesia and then in Bosnia.

In all this – applications, raising support, training, interviews – did anyone ever ask who Rob Farnsley REALLY was inside? No. I never lied. I was never asked. And my secret, which was mine alone, remained. I didn't even think how it might disqualify me or cause me problems. Had I thought about it, I still would have wondered how it would disqualify me. It never did until the end. And I question even that.

Chapter Five

From Indonesia to Croatia

"I tell you the truth, unless a kernel of wheat falls to the ground and dies, it remains only a single seed. But if it dies, it produces many seeds." – John 12:24

ON MY WAY TO JAKARTA, and then Bandung, Indonesia, I stopped off in Irian Jaya (that was what it was called in those days; now it's called West Papua Province) to visit some missionaries I had come to know, mostly via mail (remember mail? Not e-mail). Irian was the location for classic stories we have read about: cannibals, headhunters, remote villages, many unwritten languages and, of course, the first white people who arrived there as missionaries – awesome people who had given up almost everything we think we need for a good life.

While there, I have never forgotten reading John 12: 24-25. Jesus is speaking. "I tell you the truth, unless a kernel of wheat falls to the ground and dies, it remains only a single seed. But if it dies, it produces many seeds. The man who loves his life will lose it, while the man who hates his life in this world will keep it for eternal Life." Those words were challenging and gave me courage to continue on.

I certainly felt as if I had died. It was like a planned death, all those good-byes to people I thought I would never see again. I went, but it was not fun to be leaving all my oldest and best friends, with whom I had established community. Still, I did not regret it then and do not regret it now. I had a "joy set before me," (Hebrews 12:2), and I was looking forward to getting started. It still seemed like a planned death.

Two examples of heart-rending goodbyes come to mind. First, there were my surrogate "Mom and Pop." Aletha and Floyd Schelby were older by that time, already in their 70s, and I wondered whether I would ever see them again. Thankfully, I did, many times.

The second very difficult goodbye was to Justin whose story I described in Chapter Three. I cheered for him, believed in him, loved him as best I could. The cheering and believing were no different from what I do now on the deck. I was his big brother for five years. When I tried to tell him that I was leaving for the sake of the gospel, he did not understand what all that means. I often wonder how I hurt him. But he did go on. He came to faith and has continued in it, as far as I know, because we have lost touch over the past 25 years. If he sees this book and reads it, I am sure I will hear from him.

***

Looking back, now that I am at the end of my missionary journey, I see how much easier it is for people to "go," as opposed to those who "stay." I was the one to go and, though it may have been hard, I had the excitement of new challenges and adventures. Those who stay do not. They are trying to figure out how to fill the void that has been created in their relationships. It isn't easy.

A few years ago, someone who is like a son to me, Matt, left with wife and kids for the foreign mission field. I hated it. How could he do this? Has he no feelings or care for the rest of us? In some ways, he was only following in my footsteps, but that made it no easier. I have a new appreciation for real parents and grandparents and others who have let their loved ones go.

***

Planned death, or not, I left America. After a week or so in Irian Jaya, I moved on, arriving in Bandung, Indonesia, the base of the team I was joining. It was a large team, maybe 20 or so adults. At the first team meeting I attended, I felt like a ship that has come safely into harbor and ties up at the dock. I was no longer floating out on those waves, being blown who knows where. I know I shed some tears.

I lived in various places while in Bandung. I began to study the Indonesian language with a tutor and helped set up an English Center where we taught English. As I planned to spend the rest of my life in Indonesia, I went through all the adjustments of leaving home and leaving so much behind. I ached for my friends in California and longed to see them. I remember sharp pangs stabbing from my stomach up through my chest as I thought of home. If I could spend a few weeks back home and get caught up on all the happenings, would I want to return to Indonesia? I wasn't sure. But that was not in my immediate future, as far as I could tell. I did not know then that I soon would be living back in the United States.

Six months later, the mission agency asked me whether I would be willing to move to the home office and help out there. I certainly was not a key player in Indonesia, and if I could better serve the cause from the home office, I would agree to go – subject to my sending church's approval, which was given. Although I was heading back to the States, it was to the East Coast where the home office is located. What I really preferred was to return to Fresno.

***

My short time in Indonesia was good in some ways. One, I learned what it is like to be an immigrant. I had to go to various offices for visa purposes every few months. I waited in lines and was sent from here to there. I got no sympathy from the state officials I had to deal with. I feel for immigrants here in the United States. It is not easy.

Also, Indonesia became my dumping ground for all those bad feelings when a person leaves home and family for another culture. All the things I dealt with – loneliness, resentments – I was able to leave there. Years later, when I moved to the former Yugoslavia, I did not go through all those adjustments. I had already left home years before. I had lived and worked in a missionary environment for several years by then. I was more prepared for all the issues one deals with overseas. A big one was that the people in the former Yugoslavia looked like me (I thought). I did not feel like I appeared different to them. Although I know that it was easy for them to peg me as a foreigner.

***

I worked in the home office for 2½ years. In 1994, I left for another overseas assignment. More people had come to work in the home office, and I was not getting any younger. Some said, "If you are going to go overseas, Rob, you should do it soon, as it won't get any easier for someone your age to learn a foreign language." That was fine with me because I still had not had the long-term journey that I left home to have. By then, I had visited the former Yugoslavia, where a war was going on, and thought that was the place I could best serve. Making that decision took some pushing.

I had visited our teams there and knew that each wanted me to join them. But I never had the "lightning bolt" experience that I thought I needed to be sure that was what God wanted me to do. So, I stayed put, feeling I was doing a good thing where I was. Then, one of our leaders in Europe said, "Rob, why don't you just go for it and let God stop you if He doesn't want you to go." I had never heard that kind of advice before. It was always "God called me." I did come to see that if God is God, He can just as easily stop me as send a lightning bolt. I determined to go and did pray that prayer. He never stopped me.

As I considered teams to join, one factor was leadership. I was older than any of the team leaders. I thought I needed to be on a team with a leader I respected and under whose leadership I could serve. That person was Ted in Zagreb, the capital of the new republic of Croatia. Croats were still fighting the Serbs (Yugoslavia) for their independence. Zagreb was relatively safe and away from the war zone (although long-range shells did fly in for a few days). The university with its Serbo-Croatian Language Department was located there. Given that I needed to be in Zagreb for a year or two anyway, to attend language school, I might as well join that team. A new Bosnian team was forming there also, but I was not ready to join that team. I told Ted that there may come a day when I would change teams, if I thought I should head into Bosnia. That was fine with him.

So, off I went . . . to Zagreb. And thus began a journey for which I am ever grateful.

Chapter Six

My Missionary Family

"No one who has left home or brothers or sisters or mother or father or children or fields for me and the gospel will fail to receive a hundred times as much in this present age . . . and in the age to come, eternal life." – Mark 10:29-30

As I mentioned in the previous chapter, Ted was the team leader of the Croatian team that I joined. He and wife Netty had three children when I arrived in May 1994. Their family grew to a final tally of five children. The children are, in descending order, Caleb, Josh, Dave, Sara, and Abby. I became Uncle Rob to those kids.

Becoming uncle or aunt such-and-such is not unusual for singles in the missionary world. I was Uncle Rob to many. But this family is my family in a special way. We have lived much of life in close physical proximity and intensity. We started our journey together in Zagreb. From there, over the years, we lived and worked together in Sarajevo, Ontario, Canada, and then at the home office of the mission in the United States, where we have been for the last nine-plus years. During these last nine years, I was here for their high school graduations and 18th birthdays.

When Caleb, the oldest, turned 18, Ted had an idea. We – Dad and Uncle Rob – took him to Universal Studios and dinner at the Hard Rock Cafe. Then, it was on to Cigarz for his first legal cigar (I cannot say whether it was his first cigar ever . . . you'll have to ask him).

We also did that for the other boys, Josh and Dave, as each turned 18. Sarah, who had watched her older brothers, wanted the same treatment. Mom came along on that one. We recently did the same with Abby. Mom again included. And those gals were troupers. They smoked their cigars to the nub!

After that first celebration with Caleb, I wanted to start my own tradition with them and began the 21st birthday tradition. I had been accumulating lots of frequent-flyer miles, and I made this offer: We can fly, you and me, to wherever you want in the United States. I will spend a certain amount of money for car rental, motels, food, and other expenses. Caleb chose a cruise in the Caribbean, which is pretty cheap, as vacations go, so I was saving money. I offered for him to bring a friend, and he did. That was a smart decision, as Caleb and David would go to bed late and sleep in. I was just the opposite. They had a great time together, and we managed to get some good discussion time in as well.

Josh was more creative and wanted to go to the Monterey Bay Aquarium in California. That was fine. We tasted wine in Napa Valley, crossed the Golden Gate Bridge, and viewed elephant seals on the coast.

Dave chose a cruise and brought Tony. This summer, I will be taking Sarah and her friend, Betsy, on a cruise as well. There is only Abby to go. I hope I live long enough.

For holidays like Thanksgiving and Christmas, I don't wait for an invitation to join them. They are my family and I just go.

***

Ted and Netty have been like brother and sister to me. It was not an easy day when I went to their house to tell Netty my story. Ted already knew, as I had met with he and other mission leaders already.

As the boys grew up, Uncle Rob gave "scratch backs" or "back scratches," as I would say, to them. They loved it, and so did I. But now, given my admission of same-sex attraction, the question arises – what I was doing or thinking? Netty is a very protective mom and had every right to think I was some kind of pervert, despite my assurances that "nothing was going on." She received my news and me very graciously, as Ted had done.

But the cruise with Dave was coming up soon, and they wanted me to be sure to tell him and all the boys my story, which I have done. As well as the girls. They never skipped a beat. I don't think it means much to them at all. I'm still their Uncle Rob, and that doesn't change anything. The kids are scattering now, and the nest is more and more empty. A bittersweet time. It has been an unspeakable privilege to be included in their family! I am so thankful.

I have a REAL family as well. My sister has three daughters, and I am Uncle Rob to them, obviously. But after their early years and moving on to college, we have never been geographically close, and therefore have not experienced the intimacy I have had with the Eslers. Being unmarried and childless, I have been blessed to have "family" be a large part of my life.

To all my families, I thank you for your love for and acceptance of me!

Chapter Seven

The Bosnian War

"War does not determine who is right - only who is left."
—Bertrand Russell

I ARRIVED IN ZAGREB, CROATIA, in May of 1994 and began language study for a year. Learning the national language is one of the first steps in the cultural adjustments for a missionary. I quickly learned one idiosyncrasy about languages: Meaning gets lost in the translation or, in my case, in the pronunciation.

I assumed I would be "Rob" over there, like here. That was not going to work because *rob* (pronounced with a long "o,"as in "robe") means "slave" in the Serbo-Croatian language. But "Robi" (pronounced robe-ee) would work. I was "Robbie" as a kid, so I liked it. I was called Robi or, sometimes, Robert. But I liked Robi. It became a special name to me.

***

During my year in Zagreb, I had opportunities to deliver humanitarian aid to the interior of war-torn Bosnia. I remember sitting in front of my TV in the States as the war began. Not knowing anything about it at all, my attitude was . . . the United States and United Nations need to stay out of it and let those people duke it out. Whoever wins, wins. The loser will have to submit. Once I got involved there and met real people on all sides, my solution wasn't so simple anymore. I picked up lots of hitch-hiking soldiers going to or from the front. They were real people. I liked them. I didn't want them to die or be wounded.

Because there was no winner in this war (the sides signed the Dayton Agreement[6] to end the war), there were still three sides, all of which had armed themselves to the teeth. All three sides (Serbs, Croats and Muslims) thought that, given a bit more time, they could have won it. Consequently, none was too desirous of submitting to another group. Therefore, when it came to running a country with three very feisty ethnic groups, it just didn't – and doesn't – work. It makes me think of the issues in the Middle East right now.

***

My first venture deep into Bosnian territory was in late December 1994. I was going with my European leader, Mike, to search out an area he had heard about where medical equipment and supplies were needed. The hospital had been shelled, and the staff members had fled to their ethnic side. Now, they were trying to run a hospital out of an elementary school.

I met Mike on the Adriatic coast, the Croatian side, and we rented a car, a Russian Lada, a very simple, but dependable car. The Soviet Union allegedly had copied the design of the Italian Fiat. It was such a simple and dependable car that almost any roadside mechanic knew how to work on one.

On the second night, we were in central Bosnia, in a town called Kiseljak. There was a large hotel there, built for the 1984 Winter Olympics, and it was taken over by the United Nations. Mike is a smooth talker and, with a pass for himself that he got somewhere, he was able to get a Malaysian soldier to let both of us through the gate and into the hotel. Once inside, we were able to get a room and also eat at the cafeteria. The cafeteria was for the U.N. soldiers, and the food was plentiful and warm.

It was a snowy night in Kiseljak, deep in the war zone, and I was thankful to be there. Sometime in the middle of night, I was awakened by multiple shots going off. A lot of shots! I jumped up from bed, scared witless, thinking fighting had broken out right there in the U.N. compound. Mike calmed me down by saying, "Rob, settle down. It is New Year's Eve, and it just turned midnight. The Croat soldiers outside of the compound are celebrating."

---

6. Peace negotiations were held in Dayton, Ohio, and were completed December 21, 1995.

The next day, we took off, heading north through the snowy countryside. We turned onto a road that we thought we should be taking. We were flagged down by a local resident, asking what we were doing (Mike could speak his language). He told us that if we went much farther, just around the bend, we would enter Serb territory outside Sarajevo. That was the front line and our lives would be over. I drove that road so often after the war and remembered what could have happened to us. We turned around and found a better way.

Eventually, we arrived in a little town outside the big city of Tuzla in northern Bosnia – not far from where I was living in Zagreb. But in between was the war zone between Serbs and Croats and Muslims (the latter two had formed a "Federation"). So we had to go a very long way around to avoid the war zone and stay in Federation territory. Today, you can drive to Tuzla from Zagreb in four or five hours. Then it took 20 hours.

It was New Year's Day and, by that afternoon, we arrived in a small place where the doctor and CEO of the hospital lived as a refugee with his wife and children. They were Muslims who had fled Serb guns. This room was lit by one small bulb hanging from the ceiling with about as much glow as a cigarette butt. It was the only light we had as the sun set. That scene is etched in my memory. The only heat we had in that snowy place was from the wood-burning stove where they cooked. We discussed what medical supplies we had to offer, and we agreed that I would return a month or so later with a truck full of supplies.

Then they fed us a lunch, not knowing that we would ever return. Or have supplies. We ate delicious leftover chicken and potatoes, most likely the only food they had, planning to make it stretch out for days. But they gave it to us.

I found that all three of those ethnic groups are very hospitable. Certainly much more so than Americans. I am not so sure how hospitable they are to one another, but they sure were to me as a foreigner over the years. People would often ask me what the typical fare was. My answer was that I wasn't sure. I only know what they fed me. But I know that what I got was the best they could offer. I don't think they ate like that very often.

So we departed, and I realized that I would be returning somehow in a month or so. I, who could hardly say "hello" in their language, was going to return with a truck, a truck driver I didn't know and could hardly communicate with, into this snowy, cold, war zone. I left in fear and trembling!

I did return in a month with my driver, Marko, and a little yellow English/Serbo-Croatian dictionary. Marko did most of the talking as we crossed in and out of various territories controlled by Muslims or Croats. At one major border, "custom agents" saw a sucker in me and ripped me off, making me pay several hundred dollars of trumped-up fees. I was so naïve, thinking they would be so happy to receive help. But no, they wanted bribes, and I had no choice. I would handle it differently now.

We slept in the truck on the snowy sides of the road, and we would turn on the truck's engine at times to run the heater. I feared carbon monoxide gas. Occasionally, we slept in places that had beds. It is not fun getting into an ice-cold bed. When they warmed up, they were fine.

Once, Marko and I came to a territory too dangerous to pass through. Muslim soldiers (really, only young boys) warned us that just ahead Serbs were on the hillside shooting at vehicles. They said there was a U.N. convoy coming in a while and, if we fell in behind them and stuck close, we should be OK.

That is what we did, after passing several hours with these soldiers. Those young men stole my heart. They were so proud of themselves and their new country. I wanted to take a picture of us together. They were happy to do so, but not without their guns. They had to look tough. Later, before our return the same way, I asked Marko what I could take those guys. He said cigarettes. I never wrote in my quarterly newsletter to donors and others that I bought cigarettes with their money to give away as gifts.

At the customs office in Tuzla, Marko was in an official's office doing paper work. I was waiting in the unheated reception area, feeling cold and alone, and dreading the return through that dangerous area. A radio was playing in the background and, suddenly, I heard Whitney Houston singing, "I Will Always Love You." I thought, "My gosh, here I am in the middle of nowhere, cold as can be, isolated, alone, in a war zone, and there is Whitney singing this song that I love." I wondered whether she had any clue about where her songs might be sung or how they could warm the heart of some dude like me who needed to hear that I was loved and not forgotten out here.

***

After my trips into Bosnia, I decided that I wanted to move down there. How could I not? People were wide open. War tends to do that. People were so desperate, questioning all they held dear. All the old systems were breaking up. We saw, over the next years, many professions of faith. Many were not "real," as people thought they would get more aid if they came to our Bible studies and meetings. We always assured them that what we had we would share and it made no difference whether they believed or not. They said they understood this, but I don't think they did. They thought, and were sometimes right, that they would get more help if they were part of our little church.

I eventually moved from Zagreb and closer to a town I had started to get involved in – Novi Travnik. Before the war, going from Zagreb to Novi Travnik would take about five hours. At the time I lived in Zagreb, it took about 15 hours to get to Novi, as I had to drive around the front lines in a big circle, on slow roads, even in good weather. That led me to move to Mostar, about three hours from Novi. I had met another single man, David Lively, who lived there. Having Davey there made the move much easier.

There was a flat just below his that I could rent. He was with another mission organization and had just moved there himself. He became my new, close friend.

My teammates in Zagreb had families and were not prepared to move them to this unstable area. But I was single and expendable, so to speak, though being single has its advantages. I did not have a wife and kids who kept me from moving into the war zone. It was only me. My time was my own, and I always was free to move around. That served very well in Bosnia during the war.

***

I well remember my entry into Mostar. Anti-tank triangles of railroad rails blocked roads leading into town. I zig-zagged around them with my car. Just before them was this sign: Ratna Zona. The first time I went by it, I wondered: What did it mean? I picked up my little yellow dictionary and looked it up: War Zone. Wow. I was entering a declared war zone.

"Ratna Zona" was going to be the title of the book I never wrote about my journey in Bosnia. I think it refers to so many aspects of life there even today. There is a spiritual war. A political war. An ethnic/religious war of hatred. An economic war. And not much peace, although there is no fighting going on now.

***

Those early days were a tense time for me. Every time I would drive up to Novi, I had to pass through army checkpoints. The Croats and Muslims were fighting together in this loose, fragile Federation. They each had territory they controlled. As the road would go in and out of these territories, I had to go through a Croat checkpoint . . . at gunpoint. Next came Muslim territory just down the road and more guns. A while later, I left Muslim territory and re-entered Croat territory. In and out of checkpoints about six times. I never attempted to cross over front lines into Serbian territory. Serbs would have shot first and asked questions later.

Mostar had become a city divided. Croats on the west side, Muslims on the east. The Neretva River in between. There is an old bridge there, called *Stari Most* (Old Bridge). It was built by Turks during the Ottoman Empire. It symbolized the connecting of the old and new world.

A year or two before my initial move to Zagreb, and eventually Mostar, I was watching the news the night the bridge was demolished by shelling from Croats. Elderly people were interviewed through their tears as they watched their beloved symbol being destroyed. When the bridge came down, the federated Muslims and Croats turned on each other, and the war was three-sided. It was a bloody time.

***

I lived, for that first year, on the west side, the Croat side, the "New World" side. It had more accommodations. I was taken in by Davey Lively's Evangelical Church as one of its humanitarian workers. I was aligned with Baptists in Croatia, but that name made no difference to these people (it was more of a Pentecostal church). They loved me and prayed for me, and always wanted reports when I returned from a week or 10 days in Novi Travnik. They were thrilled to hear about the conversions and baptisms, as was I, regardless of the ethnicities of the new converts. The gospel had broken out there. It was amazing.

The Serbs controlled the high mountains around Mostar, and it was not unusual to hear the explosion of a shell they had lobbed down on the city. Usually shells seemed to fall on the Muslim, or eastern side, of the city.

***

After about one year, I moved to Novi Travnik. The Trajkovski family was my family there. They were husband Radovan and wife Blazenka and sons Sasha and Vladimir. When I first met them, they were refugees. They fled their flat and town when the war broke out, as they were Croats, and the town had become a mainly Muslim town. They lived in Novi Travnik (Novi for short) for the duration of the war. It was also a divided city, with Croats on the lower side and Muslims mostly on the upper. They lived there for several years and then, when the war ended, they were allowed back into their old flat. It had been occupied as well, and that person needed to leave, just as they needed to leave their Novi flat they were "squatting" in.

They were some of the first to profess faith as we started to visit Novi. On short visits, when I came up from Mostar, I stayed with them. I remember their first Christmas as believers. We were hunkered down in their little one-bedroom flat, with six or seven of us staying there. Blazenka had cooked turkey meat before, but never a whole turkey. She did that for me in a wood-burning stove/oven! I described cranberry sauce, and she made a concoction that was just like it.

It was freezing outside, but we were warm and snug in their flat. Bedtime was always a challenge. Blazenka and Radovan and Aunt Zora slept in the living room/dining area. We single males were in the only bedroom, which did not get heat. Climbing into those ice-cold sheets was always a shock. With blankets piled high, I slept warm and cozy.

***

As church-planting goes, at least in my experience, Novi was an experience that few have. In the next few years, approximately 50 people made professions of faith, and a whole lot more heard the gospel. Granted, a lot of them did so thinking they would get more humanitarian aid from us, even though we assured them what we had, we would give to all, not only to those who became Baptists. As time went on, some "converts" disappeared, but in Bosnia almost all of the fellowships still functioning were started during the war or soon after.

People are desperate during a war, and seemingly much more open to new ideas and values, seeing that their old values were empty and bankrupt. After the war ended, the three ethnic groups (Serbian, Croatian, Bosnian/Muslim) settled into their various religious traditions that identified them as a people, whether you believed or not. If you are a Croat, you are a Catholic, regardless whether you profess to be an atheist. It is simply who you are. Serbs are Orthodox, and Bosnians are Muslim.

It became a very difficult place to be a church planter. A man I respect told me years ago, "Being in the way, God used me." I am not sure that comes from the Bible. It may. I was not much else than "in the way" for much of that journey, but God did use me. What a privilege it was and how great it is now to look back at it all, although going through it had many difficult times. Memory is wonderful like that. You tend to remember the good things.

***

I moved eventually from Novi to Sarajevo for about five years, and the last town I lived in was Travnik. Not Novi Travnik. Novi means new. It was the original, and therefore old, city in the area. It was a decidedly Muslim town. I'd had bad vibes about Travnik for years as I drove through it, but in the end I had a desire to plant myself there. I went alone. Not a good idea.

Nothing spiritual, or in a church-planting way, ever happened in the two-plus years I spent there. One of the fun things, in my attempt to connect with people, was to be the host of a weekly radio show on Radio TNT. It was called "Rockin' to the Oldies with Robi." My theme song was Bob Seger's "Old Time Rock 'n' Roll." I worked my way from the first songs of the rock-'n'-roll era up to about 1980. Then go back. I featured a different group each week, like the Beatles, for example. It was supposed to be a call-in show, in English. But that never really happened. Even my good English students (I also was teaching English) were too ashamed to call in, exposing their, to them, bad English. So, I mostly talked and rocked to the oldies. Sadly, it was the highlight of my week. I wish the highlight could have been a Bible study with new believers, but it never happened.

Chapter Eight

From the Field to Member Care

Compassion is not a relationship
between the healer and the wounded.
It's a relationship between equals.
Only when we know our own darkness well
can we be present with the darkness of others.
Compassion becomes real
when we recognize our shared humanity.

— Pema Chodron

I NEVER THOUGHT TURNING 60 would be such a big deal. After all, I had gone through the major dates of turning 40 and 50, and they were just birthdays, although celebrated in a bigger manner. I thought turning 60 would be the same. I planned, and had, the most memorable party I ever had.

The party was held in an old village in the foothills above Split, Croatia, in an old stone house, with a big, vine-covered terrace, which looked out over the Adriatic Sea. Lunch and dinner were catered by the family that lived in that house. I had friends arrive from the United States, Switzerland, and various places in Bosnia and Croatia. It was awesome, eating, drinking, chatting, watching the sunset over the Adriatic, and Dalmatian music in the background, as an *a capella* men's group was practicing nearby. As is the custom there, I paid for it all. When anyone has a birthday, he is to be the one to pay for it all. I like that. No surprises whether I will have a party or not. If I want one, I do it.

In Travnik, I had no other teammates from my mission agency, and had become close to a team of about six people from another mission agency, which moved there when I did. Although I loved them and was so thankful for them, I was still lonely. I had certainly, over life, learned how to live alone in places where I had close friends close by. But in this case, I was struggling.

This was one lesson I learned about missions. In most cases, I think it is unwise to let people head out on their own to isolated places. For me, especially, I saw how much better and more effective I am when working with other people. For example, I might feel that I had visited with Samir enough. It was going nowhere. I was tired of it and would not have gone again. But if I'd had a teammate, he might have said, "Rob, let's go visit Samir today." And when my partner says that to me, I am ready to go.

I was alone in Travnik by choice. I had already lived in Bosnia for many years and thought, if anyone can do this, I can. I was frustrated with all our people being bunched up in the bigger cities, and I needed to set my own pace and go where there was no church or fellowship of any kind. I was given a long leash. In retrospect, I think I made a move that pleased me more than my Father thinking it was right. So I moved to Travnik.

Travnik was so unlike my previous experiences in Bosnia. Earlier during the war and later as it was ending, people were much more open to the gospel. It didn't really matter what flavor of religion they had. Now, years had gone by and they had settled in to their ethnic religious identities. They were not open like before. Earlier, there always was a small group that came together very fast, where we met for Bible study discussions. When that did not happen in Travnik, I saw I was a much better "fisherman" when I had a group to invite people to. I then could follow up with them to see what they thought. I just did not have that in Travnik. Moving to another town was not the answer. I would have had the same problems there.

I began to think that maybe I was a bit old (soon I'd be turning 60) to be the point person in an unreached town. I could not connect with the younger set in any meaningful way, although they loved my English teaching. Trying to connect with men or women my age was very difficult. I began to think that my singleness was playing against me. I had never thought that before.

I began to have thoughts like this: If I were donating money to Rob, knowing his ministry is ineffective, I would stop giving. Yet my donors were so faithful, and I never had a need to raise more support. All they knew was that I was in faraway Bosnia serving the Lord, and they believed in me and they gave. I became uncomfortable with that. I have given to those, over the years, that I believed in. I did not give so much because I thought what they were doing was so strategic. I have already written a bit about my belief in seasons of productivity and dormancy. That belief in me surely caused my donors to be so faithful in their giving. Yet, this time, I was not OK with it. Something had to change.

I started to pray something like this, which was the prayer I prayed as I started to prepare to move to Bosnia in the first place: "Lord, I think this journey here is over. I think it is time for me to head back to the USA. If you don't think so, fine. All you need to do is stop me. But if you don't, I am leaving." He never stopped me from going there, and He did not stop me from leaving there. As the years have gone by, I am convinced He knew what was good for me, and I have never regretted my departure.

But I sure never thought my world would come to what I thought would be a crashing end if my secret ever came out. Which it did about six years later.

***

I returned to the States, and began my tenure in the Member Care Department of my mission agency. I had been strongly recruited to join the mobilization team, but I was not interested in mobilizing more people to leave for the field. I was more interested in taking care of the missionaries we already had.

I never got any training initially in what I was supposed to be doing. I was able to find my way, and the care program gradually became more sophisticated. In some ways, what I did then, I continue to do. It is another form of "Deck Therapy" from a long distance. Missionaries occasionally came to our office and spent some time. Then we could do personal, face-to-face debriefings. I loved those. A "debrief" with a missionary, in our context, meant spending several hours in going over the last years of their time overseas. You never quite knew where the conversation was going to go, but it could cover events, personal issues, relational issues, team problems, marriage, kids, what God has been showing them, and so on. You learned to ask good , leading questions, and then stay quiet and listen. I love those kinds of conversations. I call it going deep into the heart and not so much into the head.

Our Member Care team was partly the mission's Human Relations Department for those who were overseas or on the way home. We did have to deal with some messy issues … depression, suicide attempts, unfaithfulness, pornography, much of what led to a dismissal from the agency. Now that I have had my own "crash," and the truth has come out about me, I do wonder about the way we handled some of these issues.

To the end, I loved being on the care team.

I never imagined that I, the caregiver, would be in need of some of the same tender care. In my need it seems I was shipped off to let professionals handle me. At the end of which time, I was dismissed. I felt no care was offered after I returned three months later. Some people at my church knew what was going on, and they did reach out and care for me. In my shame, however, I was not ready to reveal myself to everyone and give them the opportunity to love on me. Which I think most of them would have done.

***

During that time, before the crash, I was having dinner with a friend I had not seen in years. More of a colleague than friend; we did not know one another from social settings. As I recounted my life and what I was doing and loving (especially the deck time), he said something like, "Seems to me, Rob, that you have entered convergence." "What is that?" I asked.

I learned that convergence is a stage in later life, when life experiences and learning come together and one can use them to touch other lives. I thought, "Yes, my life has converged."

Years later, when my world crashed, I "unconverged." Now, by the mercy of God, I am on the road back. Maybe a bit different and certainly with new life experiences. I have had the biggest event in my life happen to me, the revealing of the deepest and darkest and most shameful secret I could have. I have come through it, praise the Lord, and can use even that as one more life experience in the lives of others.

Some men may see their golf game improve over the years, and in retirement they live the "converged" life playing golf. Or fishing. Or traveling. To me, that is sad. I want to live my later years touching as many lives as I can. How do I do that? By being a safe place for them to come and share what is going on. Loving them. Believing in them. Giving them courage to engage their domain in strength and love. Praying with them. Helping them wonder what God is up to when things seemingly go wrong. I may take others with me when I go fishing or travel. Mostly, though, I am staying right here, cooking meals, ordering cigars, reading books and the Bible, and touching men's lives right here on the deck.

Chapter Nine

The Revelation, the Fallout

"Hi, I'm Rob. I'm a sex addict."

— The typical type of self-introduction when one goes to any kind of "anonymous" gathering, be it alcoholics, narcotics, sexaholics, etc.

AT THE BEGINNING OF THIS BOOK, I shared how the secret came out and where and with whom. It was April of 2012. When I revealed my secret – that morning in front of the pastor and two other men at my home church in Fresno – I volunteered to go to a nearby live-in counseling center used by many mission agencies and others. I also made it clear I would rather not go there because it is only a few blocks from the church and I could bump into many people who would know me and would ask why I was there or even in town. They thought it was best to have me deal with this in the context of where I had been living for years and had an extensive support group. I liked that, and appreciated their attitude so much.

After returning home, I had several meetings with different mission leaders, and my pastor, who is also a very close friend. Those meetings led to a "monitoring team" that guided me on the next steps. I started a weekly counseling routine with a man who "specialized" in same-sex attraction. I started to attend various "sexaholic" meetings daily. They go by various names – sex addicts anonymous, sexaholics anonymous – and are fashioned closely after Alcoholics Anonymous. Every time you speak, you refer to yourself as a sex addict or drug addict or whatever. So, I became a "sex addict." "Hi, I'm Rob. I'm a sex addict."

As I said this, these thoughts kept echoing in my mind: "Why am I at this meeting and calling myself a sex addict? Because I did masturbate, and admitted it when my secret came out?

The Christian culture is pretty much one of "don't ask . . . don't tell." Oh, we admit that we "struggle with lust" sometimes. That is acceptable. But we rarely share what we are really doing or thinking privately. My generation, at least in my experience, has never talked about this. We didn't allude to it, talk about it, pray about it (other than privately), or anything else. So when it all comes out for someone, the conclusion is, he or she is perverted, and an addict. How many times a month, week, or day makes an addict? You choose.

Am I a sex addict? I am not. Do I get "randy?" I do. Do I fight it? I do. Do I always win? I do not. Have I at times been "more active" than other times? Yes.

"Sobriety" is another word thrown about in these meetings. "I have been sober for a week, month, four months, a year." And we are cheered. In some of the meetings, "sobriety" is an elusive term. For some, it means having sex with only one person, same sex or not. For others, it means they don't look for anonymous sex on craigslist. Never mind what they do with people they know. For still others, it means no self-sex at all. Only with their wives. And so on.

In the years since my revelation, I have spoken with many men, younger and older, who, once they have heard my story, say something like this: "Well, Rob, since you have been so honest with me, let me share something with you that I have told no one." If their inner secrets were known, many of these men would be sent to the same kind of counseling center I was. But don't ask and don't tell. I don't ask. I simply tell my story, and often it prompts the other person to feel safe enough to tell some of his.

I have learned that, if I want intimacy with someone, I need to be vulnerable. This new opportunity to be open has only enhanced the safety and honesty that one will hopefully find here on the deck. Vulnerability begets vulnerability. Truth begets truth.

I am not against these groups. I think they are helpful. I am not even against the concept of "don't ask, don't tell." I am against the prevailing attitude of not doing anything, and when the truth comes out about someone, then they are treated in a different manner by people who may be secretly dealing with the same issues, but are too afraid to say so. I was like that.

***

I had a very difficult meeting with about 10 of the "young bucks" who were regulars on the deck. I had been told to tell them that I had an addiction to pornography and masturbation. But not the true secret. Through all of this, I thought I was fighting to keep my job with the mission agency, so I did what I was told. After that meeting, I got nothing but love from them. Even one who said, "I still want to be like you."

In the next few weeks, as they found their way individually to the deck, we had some of the best, most open and honest times we had ever had. I thought, now that I had admitted to the same struggles they may have had at one time or another, I was looked upon as a real and normal person – not some spiritual giant who never had human, "fleshly" struggles.

***

The regimen of counseling and SSA meetings continued.

After a few weeks of this, it was decided that I should go to the more intensive, live-in counseling center in Fresno. The question had arisen in my monitoring team (I think) about what was "really" going on out on that deck. Not so much in overt, outward activity, but what was in my head. What was I really thinking? Was it "healthy"? Still hoping that this would help keep my job, I agreed.

I also was asked to have another meeting with those young bucks to tell them the true reason I was going. For me, it was a very shameful meeting and admission. Pick 10 people who look up to you in a big way, whom you mentor in one fashion or another, get them together, and then tell them the most shameful thing in your life. Your deepest, darkest secret. Does that scare you as it did me? Maybe I am so in need of respect and inclusion that I saw it differently from the way you might. I don't think so.

After that meeting, I got nothing but love, even from the same young man who whispered in my ear that he still wanted to be like me. Was he crazy? Thank you, Dan. I will never forget it!

***

One evening before leaving for the counseling center, I shared this story with someone from my mission agency's monitoring team. Why? I suppose to share some little positive thing that had happened that made me feel less rejected. The response (although denied later) was, "YOU? Why would he want to be like you?" I hung my head and thought, "Yeah, why would he want to be like a scumbag like me . . . ." Obviously, I have never forgotten this scene. I did not make it up. How could I? It was one more nail in my coffin of self-hate and doubt and shame.

I was also told by this person that I was not "broken." That would mean I was not contrite enough, not repentant enough. I wrestled with this for weeks. Was I not broken? What did it take to show that I was broken? How many tears does one shed before they are broken? Someone recently asked, "Can one be broken of temptation?"

***

Not long afterward, I attended a conference led by a highly respected Christian psychologist and counselor and author. Knowing what I was wrestling with, he called me over at the end of the week and, completely unsolicited, said: "You're broken."

Earlier, when I shared my story with him, thinking he might want me to leave the group, his first words were: "Well, you're not gay."

I had not gone to him to ask him that question. I was not looking for a pronouncement from him as to who or what I was. But hearing those words meant everything to me.

If you, reader, see yourself as gay, please forgive me. To me, "gay" means lifestyle, and I am simply not interested in that lifestyle. Maybe there will come a day when I am comfortable with that word in reference to myself. But right now, I am not. SSA is OK. "Homosexual" is the biggest stretch I can make. Even the "H" word connotes lifestyle, I think. But what else am I if not a homosexual? I don't know. I am still thinking through this.

***

As I got ready to leave for that second meeting with the young bucks to tell them the true reason for my leaving, I thought of taking some *rakija* (pronounced *RAH-key-yah*). It is brandy made in the former Yugoslavia. The makers of it are quite proud of their product. I was able to bring, and have others bring, some of it back to me. As people would come to the deck, I would offer some of this "hooch," and we would toast one another, looking into each other's eyes, and saying a Yugoslav word I taught them. *"Živjeli!!"* (ZHIV-yeh-lee, meaning "cheers" or "life"). It was a special ritual for us. Knowing I would not see them for months, I thought we could have a special toast at my departure, if this were appropriate. Well, it was not appropriate, and we did not do it, although everyone knew I had brought the *rakija*.

I shared my secret story with them, got hugs, and was dismissed to go home. One of them texted me to wait close by and said he would share a shot of *rakija* with me. Thank you, Adam! But when we met, he told me that they had been advised to leave me alone after he had texted me. I quickly left and went home. I felt so alone.

They were told this was my time when I needed space to deal with my issues – no texts, emails, phone calls, visits.

My cynical side, which is big, says, sarcastically, "Good advice. Pull in all support systems and let the sinking soul find his way." My attitude was that it was reminiscent of the old line that only the Christian army shoots its wounded. But those guys were doing what they were told would be "best" for me.

I am so thankful that, by the time this all happened, my walk with God was the best and most intimate it had ever been. Over the previous years I had come to truly know and believe that I was His beloved Son. I could have easily gone to the "Why me?" attitude, but I did not. At least for the most part. God was up to something and I was going to get to see what. At that time, the Martina McBride song "Independence Day" became a joy to sing. I was becoming more free than I had ever been.

That does not mean to say that I don't have a need to please people and want them to like me. I do. Guilt and shame were for sure playing in this mix and the enemy was alive and well. But I do believe I could see the mercy of God in it all and knew that, if this secret was ever to come out, this was the time.

***

Before leaving for the counseling center, I had a meeting with my Member Care teammates. I shared everything with them. I asked for their forgiveness for being the deceitful person I had been all these years. I heard words of love, respect, forgiveness, and best wishes captured in such thoughts as, "You'll come back better than ever."

I knew I would be gone for at least three months and the counseling center would cost me a bunch of money.

Did I say I was fighting to keep my job? I didn't hear from any of my colleagues while I was out there and, when I returned, everything had changed.

Chapter Ten

My Time at the Counseling Center

"The counselor says that with more time and more surgeries, I will begin to feel normal again. She says this with a mouth that can still smile. It's so easy to be reassuring when you have lips."

— Rasmenia Massoud, *Human Detritus*

WHAT DID I LEARN AT the counseling center? Sometimes I wonder. Even before leaving my home, I had the thought, "What are my monitoring team and mission leaders expecting? That I will return saying now I am changed? Now I deal with female images? Will that make me OK?" I don't know. That didn't happen.

It was a very lonely time at the counseling center. Here I was in my hometown, although I had not lived in Fresno for a long time. The house I still owned and rented out was only four blocks away. Although I had shared in a newsletter with many that I would be there, I had made a firm request of friends: Do not try to get in touch. I stayed away from my home church, which was less than one mile away. When I went out on the street, I wore a floppy hat and had my head down so I might not be recognized. I avoided places in the evenings where I thought I might run into people I knew. I did not have to go incognito. It was my choice. But I was so ashamed of myself that I didn't want to deal with my oldest friends and acquaintances. It was a self-imposed exile, more so for me than others who were also at the center for counseling.

Nevertheless, I did meet weekly with two men from my home church, at separate times. It was a highlight of my week.

One was a man whom I had had a large part in leading to Christ and discipled for years. With the other, I had played a big role, I like to think, in his overall Christian journey. Now, here I am, this "sicko" who needs to be at the counseling center (my view and words).

One weekend, Jim took me to his cabin in the Sierra. It was so refreshing and exciting to get away from the center and act as if I weren't a fugitive on the loose and act naturally but, of course, in a place where I would not be recognized.

After a few weeks in the "program," the other friend, Bob, said, "Rob, I think this place is great, and they do a good thing. But tell me again, why are you still here? You're still the same Rob that brought me to Christ and discipled me."

And I was. I was just more "revealed" than ever before. Naturally, I loved his thoughts. Why WAS I still here? I knew I would be here for at least three months. How did I know that? My mission team leader had said, before I left Orlando, that she thought it would take at least three months for me to deal with this. I agreed because I was hoping to keep my job.

Another highlight at the counseling center was the weekly men's group meeting. There were usually about three to six of us, depending on who was coming into, or leaving, the program. We met for 90 minutes each week. Because it was obvious all of us were there for some significant problem, we might as well be honest with each other. Why keep secrets? Some were more honest than others, but, overall, it was the best men's group, at least for sharing our "stuff," than any other group I had been in.

Then, there was the hour meeting every day with my counselor/psychologist. I did enjoy our discussions. We delved into "little Robbie" a lot. We discovered a love-starved little boy who longs for safety and security from his dad. There is no doubt little Robbie is still lurking around in my head and heart. I long to love and be loved. Sometimes I cannot express enough of my love to those with whom I want to share it. I want to say it over and over. Of course, I want to hear "I love you," or have love shown to me. But it has to be more than a rote, reflexive response of "I love you, too."

A good deck therapy question is, "What do you think God would say when you tell Him you love Him?" Most reply with something like, "I think He would say, 'I love you, too.' " Brennan Manning, in *"The Ragamuffin Gospel*," said he thinks God would say, "Thank you." As I thought about it, I knew "this is what I want to say also." I want to receive love expressed to me and not diminish it with the same, immediate response back. Usually, I say, "Thank you." I leave it there. I will be sure to express my love for them at other times. The guys who spend time with me know that, when they say they love me, and I say thanks, I value their love. But it is difficult not to repeat it right back!

***

There were days at the counseling center when I would feel stronger. Other days, I'd feel quite weak. After six weeks, there was going to be a conference call between the counselor and monitoring team back at the home office. That was nerve-wracking for me. How would it go? Would he say something that might make the team more favorable to my return or more unfavorable? Would the team members say something I would not like to hear? It was a long 24 hours for me between the two sessions with him, with that phone conference in the middle.

The next day was a "strong" day for me. I felt confident, hopeful, positive. It didn't last long. I, of course, wanted to know immediately how the conversation went. The counselor asked me about not wearing underwear under my shorts. Where did he get that idea, true though it was? Well, it was mentioned in the conference call. Shamefully, I said, Yes, I did that sometimes. It is hot and humid in the summer where I live and work. After work, I would put on shorts. Big baggy shorts. If I were to be home alone that night, I might forgo the underwear. I thought, That must be pretty perverted in his mind.

I wondered, Who told him that? Did someone see me in an exposed position unbeknownst to me? If so, why did they not say something? Did I ever intentionally do that if I knew I would have company? No. He asked whether I did that at work. I was humiliated. I was old enough to be this man's father. I had been a businessman, missionary, and teacher. A conversation like this told me I don't have the social consciousness to dress appropriately. Through my tears by that time (little Robbie was not handling this well), I told him no. I never did that. In the first place, I never wore shorts to work and, when I was at work, or anywhere else, I dressed properly. I thought, Why would such a question come up?

I have since learned that I am not such a pervert. Lots of men do this and think nothing of it. It was just so humiliating to tell this younger man that I did that. I was guilty.

There were a couple of other "goodies" that were mentioned to him about me that my colleagues apparently thought he might want to delve into. He brought them up. I could not believe my colleagues would reveal them to him without telling me first.

My strong day dissolved in a downward spiral, and that night I was as suicidal as I think I have ever been. I had it all figured out. I could slit my wrists. I didn't think it would be so painful. I could sit in the tub and just let life ebb away. No worries that someone would come too soon. No one would disturb me until sometime the next day when I didn't show up for a meeting. Even that would not trigger an immediate hunt. So, there was plenty of time for me to expire. Thankfully, I received an unsolicited call that afternoon from my friend and pastor, Curt. I unloaded on him, and I am so grateful he did call. His call, however, only distracted my suicidal thoughts. They returned in the evening.

I lay in bed that night and pondered what I might do. I don't think I was on the verge of actually getting up and going to the bathtub and slitting my wrists. Thankfully, I am not a depressed person who has these thoughts a lot. Eventually, I fell asleep and woke to a new day. For me, though, that was as serious and close to suicide as I think I have ever been. I felt betrayed, hopeless, worthless, abandoned.

***

Another weekly meeting was pastoral counseling. Those hourly meetings were OK, and I did appreciate the man who met with me. I don't think he had had much experience with someone like me, and was a bit unsure of where to go during our times. But he cared for me and respected me and did his best.

We also had a weekly potluck dinner with all those "in the program." I use that phrase, "in the program," and smile wistfully. Over the years of my missionary journey, I would return to Fresno every few years for a home assignment (otherwise known as a furlough). Several times, I stayed at a vacant apartment at the counseling center.

It is close to my church and therefore convenient. If I bumped into friends from church, I always made it clear that I was only renting the place for my visit and, of course, I was NOT "in the program." I'd laugh and make certain it was understood that I was normal. But here I was, at the end of the day, "in the program."

***

When I look at all the hours at the counseling center – I spent one hour a day in counseling, one hour a week with a pastoral counselor, 90 minutes a week watching and discussing a video series, 90 minutes a week in the men's group, and an evening potluck on Wednesdays – that left a lot of time to fill. I read a lot. My reading habits are like this: In the mornings I read Christian books. That would be followed by time in the Bible. My favorite authors are Brennan Manning, John Eldredge, David Benner, and others. The recurring theme in these writers is, as Manning would say, the furious love of God. I needed all I could get in that department. Reading the Gospels over and over also helped sustain me. I love Jesus and how He interacted with the common folk and religious leaders.

The rest of my day would be spent reading best-selling novels of one kind or another. I also met with Jim and Bob weekly for a couple of hours each.

What I am getting at is this: I question sending single people to places like the center. There isn't enough to do to fill the time, it is desperately lonely, and it is costly.

***

A highlight of my time there was a fishing trip to Alaska. I had paid for this trip months ahead, before my world crashed. I wondered whether the center would let me leave in the middle of my therapy. But a leave was approved, and I met my friend, Adam, in Anchorage. I texted him that morning to say I was a bit nervous about seeing him. He would be the first person from home I'd seen since I left in shame. His reply: "Don't worry, Rob. I love and respect you just as much as I ever have." Wow! Could it be true? We met in Anchorage, travelled to the lodge, and fished for halibut and salmon for a week. What a memory. Adam is the one helping me write this book. I am so thankful!

***

My time at the center was building toward a meeting near the end of August. As the final weeks went by, I worked with the psychologist/counselor about what I would say to my mission agency team leader who was flying out for a series of meetings with me, the counselor, a pastor from my Fresno church, and my pastor, Curt, who also was flying out. Also included were my pastoral counselor and a friend/colleague who was part of my monitoring team. My counselor and I worked quite a bit on what I would say, what I had learned, what I had accomplished.

Everyone arrived at the center about noon on a Thursday. They came into my apartment to chat for a while. It was there I was planning to share what I had worked on. All the "big meetings" were to be held the next day. The team leader (out of respect for me, she said) told me immediately that I would not be taken back onto the team. She gave several professional reasons:

The huge betrayal by me of my colleagues (I was known for always hammering people on speaking and receiving the truth in love). In addition to the sense of betrayal, agency leaders could no longer trust me and thought that I had deceived, if not lied to, them over the years.

I was intimidating and offensive to women.

There was a sea of people for whom I was to care, and I was not doing that.

I used too much email and not enough phone calls to reach out to my people.

All these criticisms suddenly materialized despite several years of "excellent" job performance evaluations. The team leader responded that no one knew what I supposedly was or was not doing. It was only after I was gone, and others were filling in for me, that they discovered what women were saying and feeling about how I treated them. When she finished, I said there was no reason for me to go into what I had prepared. As promptly as the meeting had started, it was over, and they left. Except Curt.

He had arrived, knowing what was coming down. He stayed with me at my apartment for two nights, and I so appreciated his comfort. He mainly listened to me spout off, and be cynical and bitter. He was a friend and brother. There would come a time to deal with my feelings, but he knew then was not the time.

My job and the reason for being at the center were over. My time at the center was winding down anyway, along with my money. It was time to go. I left as soon as I could after that, about six days later. I went to my sister's home in Reno, an old safe haven, for a few days before returning home.

**

I wish I could say, in some bullet-point form, the things I learned there. It was mostly a rehashing of my life. We didn't go deeply into my sexual attractions and how they came about. We didn't discuss such questions as, "Are you born with SSA or not?" We just processed my life. And it was good.

Was it worth $14,000 to do? If I had kept my job, I'd say yes. Because I didn't keep my job and because I am not sure how early in counseling that decision was made – and without my knowledge – I would say no.

I could have done the same counseling over a longer period while staying at home. I'm sure there is something to be said for daily counseling as opposed to weekly. So, it may have been more effective than I think. I am not discounting it at all. I think a good thing is done in counseling.

I think, as well, it is sad there are so few safe places within the body of Christ that our only alternative is for us to go to counselors and share our deepest secrets.

Counseling, although valuable, is very expensive, and I simply would not have invested that much money into it. I returned home with no savings and no job.

Chapter Eleven

Returning Home

"It is a joy to be hidden, but a disaster not to be found."
– Dr. Donald W. Winnicott

I RETURNED HOME ON MY 67TH BIRTHDAY, Aug. 25, 2012. I had spent the previous few days at my sister's home in Reno, and that day I drove back to Fresno and flew out. I figured it was the best way to spend a birthday, as I surely was in no frame of mind to enjoy some kind of party.

The flight back home came about three months after I had also flown back from Fresno, when my secret first came out. Although I was not particularly joyful, I was not hoping the plane would go down. I had accumulated a lot of frequent-flyer miles and was bumped up to first class for the long leg of the trip. That was a nice way to spend my birthday.

Seven years earlier, I had celebrated my 60th birthday on the mountainside above Split, Croatia, looking out over the beautiful Adriatic Sea. Looking back, even with the lonely times, life was so wonderful then. I never even considered that one day my secret would come out and I would be so ashamed. I had come a long way from there. What a contrast.

When I arrived home, Joe picked me up. He is a friend from the mission office, but we did not know each other well. On the drive home, I told him why I had been in Fresno for all those months. He, like so many others who worked on the larger mission agency team, did not understand why I had left so abruptly. A leave of absence that occurs rather suddenly tends to raise more questions than eliminate them. As he listened to my story, he was not disappointed in me or discouraged at all. Since then, we have become good brothers. He is a weekly regular on the deck. If it's Tuesday, it is "Joe day." We are Tuesday people, like Mitch Albom and Morrie in Albom's book "*Tuesdays With Morrie.*"

The next day, Sunday, I did not go to church. I was afraid I would bump into some of the elders who had been told why I was in Fresno. I wanted to meet with them and tell them my story personally, and did so on Monday night.

Sunday night, I did go to dinner at the house of my friend and pastor, Curt. It was the same place from which I had been ushered out three months before. It was a more joyful occasion but that didn't take away my apprehensions and shame. It was the first time I would be face to face with these young men since I had shared my secret with them. In front of them, Curt honored me, saying I had done all that had been asked of me, now I was back, and we move ahead, thanking the Lord for His mercy. We toasted with the most special drink I have, the previously forbidden homemade *rakija* from Bosnia. This time I was asked to bring it. That was followed by an amazing dinner of elk, which Curt had shot, and halibut that I had caught that summer with Adam in Alaska. Remembrances of that evening bring tears to my eyes every time I share it. This was the beginning of my re-education as to how those who love you will care for you and not judge you. The beginning of living life in truth with no shame. For me, seeing the body of Christ work in a way I never thought could happen. They loved me!

The road ahead was going to be long and difficult, but these brothers were all in. I remain so thankful for that.

***

What was I going to do for a job? I had started to receive Social Security and was on Medicare. My plan had been that I would continue to work at the mission agency for several more years, and salt that money away for retirement down the line. Now, I needed it. But it was not enough to live on. A friend, Ross, is a real-estate appraiser, and he offered me the perfect job of helping him in his business. I have been working with him now for more than two years. It is just part time and sort of erratic, so I have lots of retirement days.

"Retiring" was how I couched my departure from the mission agency. Unlike most who retire, I simply disappeared. There was no buildup to it. No good-bye parties. No nothing. As word about me circulates with this book and other ways, people will better understand why I disappeared. I am saddened it ended the way it did. Anyone who works with people for 23 years wants to leave in a good way. I didn't leave in a bad way, I just … retired … disappeared.

I have seen this pattern more than once over the years in various Christian contexts. Someone, in essence, is let go, but they just disappear and eventually the leadership announces they have "transitioned" off the position. We all know the truth, but it so often isn't said.

Complicating this, in my case, is that I live on the grounds of the agency. Thankfully, I was not asked to move. I am in close proximity to all of my former colleagues of the larger agency. That used to be really difficult and still is, to some degree. Now, three years later, I have sat with many and briefly told them my story and why I retired. This proximity and intertwining of social relationships has made for some forced growth on my part. Would I not go to some function knowing some of my former colleagues would be there? At the beginning, no, I would not go. I am doing better now, but I still feel an awkwardness sometimes when I might be in a common room with some people.

Forgiveness. I wrestle with this word all the time. Have I forgiven those I think have wronged me in some way? I think so. I know that as I have asked for forgiveness, it has been offered to me. Does that mean I want to socialize with them? No. They probably feel the same way about me. I have no problem with the thought of sharing eternity with them. Sharing time with them right now? I'm not so excited about that. Even writing this book is hopefully therapeutic for me. I am a work in progress.

***

I resumed my weekly counseling with the same counselor that I had started to meet with before going to the counseling center. My Fresno church paid for about four months of counseling with him. When its donations were drawing to a close, there was no way I could continue to pay for it myself. There was nothing left to deal with anyway. People knew me. I had no secrets anymore. Counseling came to a stop.

I really did like my counselor. At the end, he said people like me usually need about four years to deal with issues like mine. I thought, four years!? To what end? I have already said that I never felt there was any agenda of helping me become heterosexual. Why in the world did someone need four years? I have such a great support system and everyone knows my story, so why would I need four years of counseling? While that may be true, and even if I agreed, I simply could not afford it.

I was starting to find truth in the quote at the beginning of this chapter. Now that I am "found out," I think it would have been a disaster if that had never happened. Why? Because I am free. Oh, I would have loved it if the crash never came. I would have chosen that, had I any control. Now, I love being loved by people who know all my "stuff." I still can't quite figure out how those who knew me before can be so accepting and loving. I hope I would be like them if the tables were turned, but I still wonder how they can seemingly love me as they do.

Chapter Twelve

Acceptance/ Estrangement

"You don't walk away to prove your worth. You walk away because you allowed someone else to dictate your value and you found yourself believing it."

— Shannon L. Alder

DISCUSSING RELATIONSHIPS AFTER MY DISMISSAL from my mission agency is tough to write about because I know there will be other views. All I can say is, this is my experience. Others are free to rebut in any way they want. Their views could even be correct, as far as facts go. Again, all I can do is write about my feelings.

When I returned to my home from the counseling center, I thought I had two "corporate" entities in my life. One was my church and the other was the mission agency for which I had worked for 23 years. Both espoused a high value of grace. But I wondered, where I would actually experience that grace, if at all? I had lost my job, so I don't know what I was hoping for there. Somehow, I did not think the grace would come from the church. I was wrong.

I met with the elders that first Monday after returning, and shared face to face what I struggled with and where I had been. I received "nothing but love." It is a phrase I will use many times, and I experience it often as I continue to share my story with people. The elders have allowed me to continue to direct our church mission committee, and the committee members have affirmed me as well. When

I shared my secret with all of them and offered to step down, they wouldn't have it. I also help to lead the men's ministry. Me? In men's ministry leadership? God is merciful, and He has a sense of humor![7]

***

I had already been asked to resign from the Member Care team, and I did. I did not resign from the mission agency. It was suggested that perhaps I could find another place within the mission to work, but there was no place else I wanted to work other than caring for the members.

I knew, more than ever, that there were many men who lived with dark secrets and had no safe place to share them. Not that just sharing is the answer. It is a start. We need safe places to do that. Those safe places are hard to find. Could I do something in that area? But that would fall into the area of the team from which I was asked to resign. That team's leadership was not interested in having me back. A close friend within the mission advised me not to leave too quickly, because I did have a lot of helpful experience that I could share. I was thankful for that, but his idea didn't go anywhere.

It seems that most people who find themselves in tough places like mine and still do not want to leave their agency are given an option. Resign or be fired. Because most of them are younger, and do not want a firing on their résumés, they resign and quietly disappear. My résumé days were far behind me. I was going to need a job. I also knew that, whatever I found at this stage of life (age 67), I would find because of someone I knew, not because of my résumé, blemished or unblemished. So, I never did resign; I just faded away. I did find the perfect job.

***

Recently, I was contacted by the wife of one of the couples I served. She did not know why I retired. She saw me on Facebook and wanted to thank me again for my service to her and her husband at a tough time. Could I come up with a bunch of other women who might say something similar? I think so. Could I come up with the opposite? Probably so. I have asked people who have worked with me in debriefs if I come across as intimidating to women. They say, "no." One

---

7. The prepared message Rob gave to his church can be read in its entirety in Appendix A.

example was given of a woman who said I intimidated her. Someone else, who has sat with this same woman said that he guessed he intimidated her as well. Worthy of dismissal? I don't think so. Not in and of itself. What I am saying is, if you felt betrayed by me and couldn't accept it, fine. Dismiss me because of that. Not for professional reasons that I was never given a chance to improve upon. Again, I had nothing but "excellent" reviews in the years previous. Sour grapes? Probably so. The offending person (me) is always looking for more grace. The offended people are probably thinking they have given more than enough. I know I asked, in my departure interview, if grace and flexibility had been given to me. The answer was "yes." I wanted more, and they felt they had offered enough.

***

I have to distinguish between people and friends who are in the mission and the mission itself. As I have met with mostly men within the mission (and some women) and shared my story, I have received nothing but love. I want to be clear in saying that it was not the whole organization that I was dealing with. It was my team within the larger organization.

It would have been nice to be sought out a bit after I got back, from people who, before my departure, had various expressions of love and respect for me, like the one saying that I would return "better than ever." But it has been silent.

***

Although this is no one's fault, it was sad for me that I did depart the mission agency with no warning. I would have liked to have said, "I will be retiring at the end of the year," and build up to it, and then it is natural. I was asked whether I wanted a farewell at the large, weekly team gathering. I said no. How do you celebrate being let go from something you have given 23 years of your life to? Again, I don't blame or point a finger at anyone over this, except maybe myself. I just wish it could have happened in a better way.

As I moved ahead, the road was a bit unclear.

Chapter Thirteen

The Church and SSA

"Or do you not know that the unrighteous will not inherit the kingdom of God? Do not be deceived: neither the sexually immoral, nor idolaters, nor adulterers, nor men who practice homosexuality, nor thieves, nor the greedy, nor drunkards, nor revilers, nor swindlers will inherit the kingdom of God." — 1 Corinthians 6:9-10

PRAY FOR ME! I want to deal with the church and same-sex attraction in love. I think I am speaking for most people with SSA by saying that I have never felt safe in admitting my sexual orientation to the church, in whatever form that could take. Let's just say any group of "organized" Christians.

While I have been involved in evangelical churches and ministries most of my adult life, these were not safe places for someone like me. I am being blunt, but honest, about this. I see newer and older churches with "grace" in their names . . . River of Grace, Amazing Grace, Grace Church of (fill in the city), ABC Grace.

I wonder how most people would define "grace." Can you define it? In years past, if I had to come up with an alternate word for grace, I would have chosen either mercy or love. Good words. But they are not grace. This is not original to me, but now I would say the alternate word is "acceptance." Actually, "risky acceptance." God "risked" in a big way when He came to us.

Risky acceptance, to me, might have looked like this if my former teammates had said:

"Rob, this is really weird and awkward for us. We don't quite know what to do with you. You really wounded us. But we still want to try to have you be a part of us. You do have something to offer, even in your deceit and supposed addictions. You have served faithfully for 23 years. We do have men (and women) with secrets, and it might be that, as you share your story with them, they will come to you as a safe place. We are not saying this is a done deal. We will be keeping our eyes open, so to speak. But we do want to go on a risky journey with you and see where we end up."

That, to me, is grace. I wish that it had been extended to me, and not just me. I wish that it might have been extended to several others who came back from overseas to be "restored," but who simply disappeared or were given the option to resign or be fired. I wish more risky acceptance could have been extended in some of those situations.

More than mission agencies, the church also needs to have the same attitude. We don't offer grace only when people toe the line. We offer grace. Period.

***

As I openly share my story with people, I often hear the comment that "we are all sinners." People say this, wanting to be kind and supportive, and wanting me to feel better. I push back though. Yes, we are all sinners. But having SSA is not a sin. Who I am is not a sin. In fact, this is not what makes me who I am. I am a beloved son of God. Just because I admit that I struggle with SSA, don't try to make me feel better by saying that we are all sinners. It is what we do with who we are that may be sinful.

The Apostle Paul admits an ongoing struggle in his life. Referring to himself as wretched and having a sinful nature. His "besetting" sin. Does this have any connection with his "thorn in the flesh" in 2 Cor. 12? I was always taught in my earlier years that the thorn had something to do with his eyes. It may have, but I don't think it was a physical problem. In Romans chapter 8 we read of the freedom he knows in Christ. There is no condemnation.

I go to Psalm 139 and read that I am fearfully and wonderfully made. I was knitted together in my mother's womb. All my days were ordained for me.

Think of a 22-year-old who is struggling with SSA and sitting in the congregation. He or she does not want to act on it. The person wants to live a life honoring to God. I know there is a lot of debate as to what that might look like these days. That person also longs for intimacy and relationship. Where is he or she to find them? These are people who need to be honored for living a celibate life. Not shamed. These people need to be told, "You will be Uncle Rob to our kids." Maybe even Grandpa Rob.

My heart goes out to these people. I have to say that I am not the best representative for this struggle of choosing celibacy, as I always thought I would get married. I did not have to make the choice at age 21 that I would live a celibate life. I kept hoping that, somehow, I would find the right one who would get me "over the hump," so to speak. I did not see myself as choosing a life of celibacy even though, as I went through life, I have been celibate.

I have been honored many times for "withholding" myself. The truth is that, due to whatever circumstances, I simply am not interested in having sexual experiences with anyone, male or female. I remain celibate because that pleases me. It has been easy. That is not the norm, I know.

I was glad to be celibate, as I had no confidence that I could perform anyway. I have had an awesome life. I did not sit around waiting to get "healed" or married before diving into ministry and into the lives of others. I have taken advantage of my singleness. Nor do I sit around waiting for others to invite me over. I have them over to the deck, or wherever I have lived. Sometimes I invite myself there, offering to bring the steaks or whatever. Unlike married people, I have had time. I have used my time.

I always had hope that I would, somehow, be freed from this same-sex attraction.

***

Recently I was with a friend. I had discipled her husband (now deceased) many years ago. She was saying how he loved me. How she loved me. How I loved him and them. How I had loved so many others, and they loved me. She said that, in her view, I loved men. Not in a sexual way. I simply loved men and poured my life into them. After first feeling a bit awkward about a statement like that, I decided it is true. I do love men. I don't dislike women, but I simply love men and I want to be involved with them.

Consider these two scenarios:

A married man comes into a church and says he loves men and wants to disciple them. He has a proven track record.

A man struggling with SSA (the people know it; he is open about it) comes into the same church and says he loves men and wants to disciple them. He also has a proven track record, although his secret just recently came out (as mine did).

Who most likely will be invited onto the men's ministry team? Thankfully, there are many churches that would not discriminate. But I think the church, overall, still has a long way to go in this area.

Chapter Fourteen

Deck Therapy

"Oh, it seemed like a holy place, protected by amazing grace
And we would sing right out loud, the things we could not say . . ."
– "The Sad Café," The Eagles

IN THE PREFACE, I REFER to "deck therapy"[8] occurring on my deck. That has become a well-known term in my circle of life. Although some people may visit me just to visit, more often than not, someone will ask whether they can come over for some deck therapy. That means that they come to talk, enjoy a beer or whatever else they may want. Maybe smoke a cigar. Generally we have a meal. I am pretty good at the barbecue. Seems I go through one about every two years, as I cook on them five times a week on average. And we talk . . . .

I have a prayer for my place that is posted at the entry. It comes from "*The Hobbit*":

"Frodo was now safe. . . . The house was, as Bilbo had long ago re-ported, 'a perfect house, whether you like food or sleep or storytelling or singing, or just sitting and thinking best, or a pleasant mixture of them all.' Merely to be there was a cure for weariness, fear and sad-ness." J R R Tolkien, "The Hobbit."

That is my hope . . . that people will feel, as we chat, that they are safe. That truth and honesty are spoken here. That what is shared on the deck stays on the deck. That weariness, fear, and sadness fall

---

8. Conversational questions used on the deck are in Appendix B.

from their shoulders. I am thankful to say that I know those things do fall. I have heard it from people many times.

Some of my brothers, years ago, took that prayer, along with a picture they took of me on the deck doing a cigar in a laid-back position, feet up, and framed it. I remember the day they gave it to me. I cried. It is the prayer that hangs by the entry. What a memory. Thanks, Jaki and Bretticus!

***

How did it all start? I certainly did not come here in 2006 with the intent of beginning a life of deck therapy with young bucks, or old. I have always, in my Christian journey, been involved with one-on-one discipleship. And it has pretty much been a life of doing that with men my own age, or a bit younger. That is what I set out to have and do and live here at age 60. But I never had a name for it.

One day, a few months after my arrival, my pastor and good friend, Curt, contacted me with a question. A young man had come to him, asking whether Curt might direct him to an older man in the church with whom he might get into a mentoring relationship. It had been suggested to him to do so by a campus worker for Cru (formerly Campus Crusade for Christ). Curt had a couple of men in mind and contacted us to see whether we would be interested. I said that I would be, and that if Matt (whom I thought I knew by face, but was not sure, as he had an identical twin, Mike) were interested in me, he would need to contact me and not vice versa. Not long thereafter, he called. After a brief chat, we agreed that he should come out one evening for us to get acquainted. He would have to come to me, because I was not going to him.

Why? My feeling was, and is, that if people are serious about discipleship they need to do some things that are not convenient for them. Along with that, I simply want to meet in a quiet place where there are no distractions. Restaurants and homes with roommates are not conducive to deep sharing.

If he came, I would cook dinner for him, as he would have to pay for gasoline and road tolls. And he came. We had dinner, sat out on the deck, and got to know one another a bit, and I proposed that, if we were to continue, we needed "rails to run on" and that maybe we could do some basic Navigator study guides together (the Operation Timothy program that I described in Chapter Four). That seemed fine to him, and we agreed that he would come the next week for dinner.

I ordered the books. There is a memory verse associated with each lesson, and I am a stickler for that. You didn't memorize the verse? OK, we can sit and chat tonight, but we will not do the lesson. I was not "graceful" in that respect! Thankfully, Matt loved to memorize, and it was not a problem for him. At that time, he was 20 and I was 60.

There are 12 lessons in two books, and we finished in about four months, as there are always times when you cannot meet, or when you do meet, there is something else to discuss. As time went on, some of Matt's roommates came out, having heard about this "old dude" that he met with. Word got out to other young men in the church and elsewhere. Often they came in pairs or small groups. Many found they wanted to have some "alone" time with me, and we set up times for them to come. As time went on, some became weekly regulars, some occasionally, and some never returned. Generally, when they came, they came for dinner.

I learned about cigars and pipes at that time. They were all into it. Not everyone, but many. I had smoked a few cigars in recent years, but not often. When guys came, they often brought some. Now I have two humidors of cigars that I keep well-stocked. You want to have a conversation with someone, young or old? Do a cigar with them. You have about 1½ hours to sit there, and you might as well talk. Through all this, deck therapy evolved. I jokingly say that I am the only "full service" deck therapist in Florida. Maybe in America. Food, talk, smokes, drinks . . . I do it all. And the view!

***

The lake I live on is not a large lake. It is, however, big enough for water skiing, wakeboarding, sailing. It is surrounded mostly by private homes. The section where I live is a RV campground and has been there for decades. It contains pads mostly for RVs. There also are a few mobile homes that were placed here, who knows when, and I rent one of those. My neighbors come and go through the year. The winter season fills the place with "snowbirds," who generally come for five months from up north. They are the most consistent community, with all the same people coming to the same places, doing the same things year after year. The rest of the year, people come and go.

As I sit on the deck facing east, I enjoy the sunrises, moon rises, storms blowing across the lake, awesome rainbows, occasionally an alligator or otter. A bird feeder hangs there to attract cardinals, although it attracts a lot of other birds as well. Whenever a cardinal shows up, I think that God is saying to me, "Rob, I like what is going on right now. I am affirming you and loving you." It is amazing to me that, although the cardinals are just coming for food, they seem to come at a moment I am thinking some thought or deep in a conversation with someone and, for me, that means God likes the thought or conversation. Everyone who has been to the deck knows of my love for cardinals and what I think they mean.

I have often wondered, if I did not live here, would people still come to see me? If I lived in an apartment and had a small balcony, would people still want to come over? I think they would, but all agree it is nice to be on the deck. It also helps to keep us from looking right at each other, as you might do in a restaurant. Sometimes there are those awkward pauses. Silence. Both our chairs will be facing the lake, and I think that helps for comfortable conversation.

***

A few years into the deck therapy journey, I tried something different. There was an old diner next to the property where I live. It had an outside patio. I asked my friend, Mike, whether he would want to work with me on creating a monthly evening with guys. It ended up being a very loose gathering of guys on the first Friday of the month. It was called the "Bible and Brew." B 'n' B. We voted and the guys did not want a formal study time. They just wanted some "hangout" time with brothers in Christ. Discussions might lead to the Bible or maybe not. Guys would come and maybe bring friends. They brought their own cigars and pipes, and could order dinner and drinks from the restaurant. Mike and I even made T-shirts with a mug on the front and "What would Jesus brew?" on the back. The B 'n' B ran its course and eventually died a slow death. It was great while it lasted.

***

During those early months of life on the deck, a good friend had urged me to go to a weekend men's retreat up in Alabama. It was called "Battle for Men's Hearts." "Battle," for short. I loved it. It was about a 10-hour drive to get there. I went several times and took others. Over the three-night weekend, there were lecture sessions and then much time spent in small groups. One could be placed in a small group at random, or, if guys came with a group, they would be together. I wanted to be more involved in the whole ministry, but often was told by group leaders that, although I offered much in the groups, it seemed I was holding something back. Consequently, they were hesitant to give me my own group to lead, unless I brought a group. I denied I was holding back, but I knew....

Through the Battle, I became aware of books by John Eldredge, Brennan Manning, David Benner, and others. I had read *"Wild at Heart"* once, but didn't want to get too deep into it. I never like books that are all the rage for the moment. But before the Battle, I read it again. Amazingly, it spoke to me. Since then, I think I have read every one of Eldredge's books many times over. I am not ashamed to say I really like John! In some circles, he would not be that popular. I like him. As well as the other writers mentioned above, and others.

As I have read and re-read these books, about ten or so, I have underlined various comments and turned them into questions to use in Deck Therapy. Simple things like, "What are you longing for these days?" Or, "As you grew up, did you feel as if you were the apple of your dad's eye?" Around eighty percent or more of the men I meet answer that last question with a "no." Including me. I have created a document of six pages titled "Deck Therapy Questions," with the book titles and page numbers, so one might go to the book to see the context. You can find the questions in Appendix B.

The other thing I took away from the Battle (along with much else) is this line: "Engage your domain in strength and love." It is my mantra. I sometimes don't do a very good job of it myself, but it still is what I so often say to those who come. Strength and love. They need to be together. One without the other does not work well. I think every man who has been on the deck more than twice knows this line. We pray for it all the time. I like it when I am giving the "strength and love" charge to another person. I don't like it so much when I need to hear it myself, which I often do.

The Battle was a great experience. I went over and over. I am forever grateful for the things I learned there, and how my heart was opened wider than ever before. Even though I was not totally honest with them.

I also bought a set of Eldredge's "Wild at Heart, Band of Brothers" DVDs. I had wanted to bring the Battle back to where I live, but that did not work out. Then I heard of the DVDs and decided I would give them a try. My place is "cabin-ish," and I thought I could hold a weekend right here and save some money for lodging somewhere else. These groups could not be any larger than four or five. That is all my place can accommodate. Even then, someone would have to sleep on the floor. In the DVD series, there are eight videos, along with suggested clips from movies like "Braveheart" to use as introductions. So, my first time around, I had four young men from church, all married, but without kids. They brought their sleeping bags and toilet articles, and everything else was here. I did charge them for food.

It was an exhausting weekend for me. I cooked, cleaned dishes, facilitated all the discussions, for the weekend. I had not planned any other activities. The videos start with some adventure . . . fly-fishing, rappelling, white-water rafting, skeet shooting. I didn't have any of those figured out, but on Saturday of the weekend, one of the guys said, "We should do one of those things." But what? Ryan said, "My parents live about 20 minutes away from here and have over 20 acres of pasture in the back. Dad has a skeet launcher." Adam said, "I have the guns and can get the clay pigeons." So we went skeet shooting that afternoon. Adam also had assault rifles (guns are his business), and he brought them. I had never shot an AK-47 before. But I have now! It was a great day, followed with steaks and cigars that evening. That part was planned. Saturday night is banquet night.

The retreat lasts from Thursday night until Sunday afternoon. The result of that weekend was a Band of Brothers that has been meeting monthly for about six years. Although I had only planned to facilitate the weekend, I am a part of that BoB. Since the first group, I have had two other weekend retreats with three to four guys each time. They also have been awesome times. Ryan and Adam have come to each one on Saturday, so we could do the shooting. Some good friends in California (my West Coast BoB) have done a weekend themselves with some younger men in the church, and it, too, was awesome for them. I did envy them as they had a team of four doing all the work for the young men. I think it is such a great example for older men in the church to be serving younger men in this way.

Here's an email I got from one of the men who came to a retreat here:

Hey man,

I know I have said thank you for doing the Band of Brothers weekend. I just want you to know that it was life-changing. The three of us have drawn very close to each other and give each other courage all the time. I am learning to give Hannah courage at a whole new level and lead her in strength and love. Our marriage is so much better in just these few short weeks.

God has been answering many prayers and doing a number on my heart and mind. It is just incredible. It is incredible to really believe I am His beloved. It is also amazing to see how the enemy has been attacking and telling me lies, but God moves through my BoBs at the right time to give me courage and remind of who I REALLY am.

I am learning to be bold and dangerous. I have even noticed in my prayers that I don't pray for protection from the enemy that much anymore. Instead I am asking to be bold and dangerous and empowered to defeat my enemy.

Life is a roller coaster, and this is a pivotal growing season for me, and I am excited to see what God does with this new growth for His glory.

Thank you so much for your mentorship, your friendship, and brotherhood.

Love you, bro!

I wish I could do more of these weekends, but I don't know quite how to get the word out further. Anyone can do them. You should try! The "how to's" are fully explained when you buy the set of DVDs.

***

As I am writing this, we completed another BoB last Friday evening with the group I have been meeting with for more than six years: Ryan, Rodney, Shaun, Brett, Adam and myself. Generally, after we have gone around sharing what is going on in our hearts, it usually ends up that one person is the center of attention for a good while. It may have come out of what he shared from his heart. In this case, it was a business decision and opportunity that could be great, or not so great, down the line. We listened, the brothers asked some very pertinent questions, and it was a very helpful processing time. I mostly observed in this one case. I realized that I am so honored to be a part of these men's lives. I have watched their kids arrive, in some cases after several miscarriages. One brother has lost his baby daughter. Jobs have come and gone. I am watching them live their lives and grow as men, and it is such a joy. And it is the same way with all the other men who come here. I am almost 70 years old. I am not going anywhere professionally any more. I don't even want to. But I really do like being a part of younger men's lives as they are "moving up" in their journeys. I pity older men who are not involved with a younger man or two. You do not know what you are missing.

A special memory for me was when one of the young bucks came out with his dad. We were doing cigars after dinner. About four of us altogether. We started on some of the "questions."[9] What are you afraid of? What are you longing for? To watch this father and son look at and listen to each other was great. I doubt they had ever answered these kinds of questions between themselves. They learned things, I am sure, they never knew. I have done the same thing with this same guy and his older brother. Are you a father of sons? Have you ever shared with them what you are afraid of these days? What you long for in your heart of hearts? Have you ever asked your son(s) these same questions? Most dads and sons don't go there. Sad.

In a self-centered way, I am glad they don't go there. That makes the young men who come all the more open and desirous of that kind of talk and affirmation with me. Even if sons have a great and open relationship with their dads, there is still a need for other, older men to help raise them. There very well may be some kinds of things young men don't want to talk with their dads about. I am thankful to be able to play that role with them.

***

I mentioned my West Coast BoB. I made periodic trips to the Fresno area, especially while supporters were donating to my mission. Although that part is over, I still go out there. Something that usually happens is a weekend in the mountains with those guys. Last year, during that time, I challenged them to consider doing a Wild at Heart/Band of Brothers weekend with some younger men at our church. They did, and I mentioned above how well that went.

---

9. The complete list of "deck therapy" questions are in Appendix B.

Another thing I did last year was to share my same-sex attraction story with them. They showered me with support and honor. They are now on track to do another Band of Brothers group during the winter.

I love being with my West Coast BoB and renewing our friendships. We relive our time in Bosnia when they came to conduct business seminars to help me connect with Bosnian people. We have many fond memories and stories. The food and drink, the translators ... my friends, who spoke no Bosnian, thought the translator was doing a great job. I asked how they would know? They looked at each other and burst out laughing, as they wouldn't know. She just seemed like she was doing it right. *Rakija*, of course. We all love the *rakija* and the toast of *"zivjeli!"*

They have once again asked me to fly out and help them grow. When I get invitations and affirmations like that, it is hard to accept and believe. I know they love me. I know they think I have lived an effective life, reaching out to many people. But now they know that I struggle with SSA. How can they think that I can help them grow? These are my words and thoughts and struggles. I say I am comfortable with myself, but still ... Me? Help THEM grow? I still have a ways to go.

I am preaching to myself when I say you don't have to have your life all together to be a mentor/discipler. Mainly, you need to be available. Will there be questions and ideas that I am not able to answer? For sure. Just admit it and say that you will do some study in that area before the next meeting. There is no shame in not having all the answers. Actually, it is probably refreshing to the other man. I WILL go out there and do my best to help them grow ... just as they help me grow in different ways.

***

When I ask the "what are you longing for these days?" question, the most common answer about 80 percent of the time concerns wanting intimacy. Not physical intimacy. Relational intimacy. We want to know and be known. We want to love and be loved. And not just by our spouses. It is not as if married men don't give me that answer. The percentages are the same. But they need a safe and open environment for them to reveal that longing.

A word of warning to you older men. I mention this elsewhere, but will do so again. If your life was like mine, you never did and never do talk about certain things. Like masturbation. These days, young men, I have found, are not like that. I discovered early that they struggle with this (and pornography) and are not afraid, at least with me, to discuss it. Before my "crash," I pretty much presented myself as an old duffer who didn't struggle with this anymore. I am "clean." But I am happy to help you! Well, post-crash, I admit I am just like them. It doesn't get any easier the older you get. But the church is pretty much in the "don't ask, don't tell" mode. Especially for older men. So, be ready for it, and maybe have an idea how you would respond to it. But be real.

If you have further questions about deck therapy, you might go to my website, *www.decktherapy.com.* You can post questions or reflections there.

At the end of an evening, guys know that we head inside and drop on our knees for some prayer time. Some "knee action." If they are new, they may say nothing, though most men do. This is a very important time. It brings closure to an intimate evening. Guys want to thank God for it. They want to do it humbly. We all pray in groups, more than likely, but rarely do we get on our knees in the various places we pray. It sometimes seems to me as if we are coming to God on our terms and not His. Praying on our knees does something. It is funny, too, how some of these "surfer boys" have trouble with their knees. Our BoB usually ends so late that some of the guys just stand, for fear of falling asleep, which has happened. But no one sits in a chair.

One last thing I remember. I mentioned Matt at the beginning. I well remember when, after several meetings together, he left one night and I looked at my watch. He had been with me for five hours. Five hours with me! Time flew by. I was amazed that some young buck would want to spend that much time with me at one sitting. Maybe I really had something to offer.

Chapter Fifteen

Grampa Robi

The only thing you take with you when you're gone is what you leave behind. — John Allston

MATT WAS 20 AND A JUNIOR in college when I met him. He lived in a house not far from the University of Central Florida campus with his twin brother, Mike; their best friend, Paul; and various other students who came and went. I always met with Matt at my place. After some months, I went to his place to have a dinner that he fixed. After dinner, we planned to go to the campus so he might show me around.

When I arrived at Matt's house that night, Mike was there, studying. I don't know that he had even been informed that I was coming, but it didn't matter as everyone seemed to fend for themselves as far as meals went. Mike did know me, although I did not know much about him. He had a question or two for me. Bible-related questions. He found my answers to be interesting, partly because I did not answer them as a theologian, which I am not, but like an old ex-missionary who probably spouts off too much. At any rate, he found my answers intriguing and, dare I say, real. Later, he asked Matt what we talked about over on the deck. Matt said that we talked about the Bible, life, stuff . . . whatever. Mike was curious and wanted to come over himself.

About a year later, Matt was leaving for about eight weeks on a short-term mission trip. I asked Mike whether he might like to come over, as I wasn't going to have Matt around for a while. Or maybe he asked me. At any rate, Mike wanted to come over while Matt was gone. We had great times as well. When Matt returned, Mike came on one night and Matt on another.

A year or so went by, and Matt and Mike got engaged to wonderful ladies, Breanna and Mandi, respectively. Mike was to be married first, in the spring of 2008. But things happened in the winter of 2008, and they put the wedding off for one year. Matt and Breanna did get married that spring. Matt asked me whether I would be a groomsman. Now, amid my insecurities, I can dismiss this and say that they just needed one more male body to match the ladies. But so what? Matt had lots of other friends he could have chosen. But he asked me, a 62-year-old, to be up there with him and the other young bucks. I had long since given up the idea that I would be a groomsman again in anyone's wedding. I had done it enough and it was always great, but those days were over. Then Matt asked me. I immediately agreed but told him several times that should he change his mind, I would totally understand. He never did.

We had the bachelor party, at least the first night of it, at my place. Thirteen guys sleeping all over this single-wide mobile home. I went to bed before they did, as I did not want to see my place dismantled for sleeping purposes. The next morning they were all over the place ... floor, beds, sharing single couches, one head on one end with feet close by, and a head at the other with another pair of feet close by. It was a sight to see. It took days to clear the air of stale cigar smoke.

The next day was spent here as well, riding jet skis, eating, doing guy stuff. A great day. The next night, which was the night before the wedding, was at Matt's place. Matt is great with words, and for bachelor gifts he had a special gift that included a framed picture he selected for each of us, a name (such as warrior, friend), and words on the back of each picture explaining why he chose the special names he gave us. He read those words out loud as each man received his gift. As he went around the room, I think I was last. What name would he have for me? I had no idea. Then, he said ..., "Father." It is one of my most treasured possessions. Words of affirmation HAS to be one of my "love languages" for sure. The note – though I won't share what was written – has them, too, along with the words of fatherhood.

Mike and Matt's dad died when they were in their upper teens. They have a great step-dad, Garry, and he has been there for them. But for some particular reason, Matt used that for me. Me ... Rob ... who is

NEVER going to have children ... never be a father ... and not because I chose a celibate life merely out of devotion to God or something.

To this day, I sometimes use the terms "dad" and "son" with Matt and Mike. I try to be careful not to go too far into that, as that is, to me, sacred territory for all of us. I don't want to push myself, because of my needs, into that "fathering" area. But they are seemingly OK with it. Just the other day, I got a text from Matt, who is half way around the world, saying it is good to be a brother and a son. He sees himself, for sure, as my brother in Christ. He also sees himself, in many ways, as my son. He has made it clear, however, that I am not his dad, and it is difficult for him to go there. I do refer to Matt and Mike as the sons I never had.

***

About a year later, after Matt's wedding in 2008, the same scenario was re-lived as Mike and Mandi got married. Again, I was a grooms-man. By then I was 63. Mike was 23. Bachelor party, jet skis. All over again. With a special memory gift from Mike. How honored can an old duffer like me be?

A year or two after Matt got married, he wanted to get a smaller wedding ring, as his was a bit too large. We were chatting on the deck, with Breanna, and the ring came up. I wear no rings. After my mom died, I got her gold wedding band, which I wore. But I lost it and had not worn any jewelry since. I looked here and there for a ring, but it needed to be special. They had come over for their Christmas dinner with me when we had this conversation.

Some days later, what do you think I got as a gift from him? The ring. It is one of my most treasured material possessions, along with the groomsman wedding gift and a few other things. All the others sit on a shelf where I go and reminisce. The ring is always with me.

***

I remember joining Mike and a bunch of his friends for a Fourth of July excursion. I always wonder as I meet their friends, "What do they think about an old man like me joining their young party?" I mentioned it to Mike in the car. He said something like, "Well, I tell them you are the No. 1 player on our team." I was happy. When I reflect on that, post-crash, I wonder what he would say. That is my "little Robbie" showing up with self-doubt.

Then, the babies started to arrive. Mike and Mandi were first. I have been around many times when my friends have had babies. I am "Uncle Rob" many times over. I love that and am honored by that. I assumed that would happen again. But no. Mike and Mandi asked me whether I wanted to be "Grampa Robi." Well, what would the other, REAL grandfathers think? I never seem to be able to accept things like this. I always have to wonder what other people will think. But that is what happened. Now I am Grampa Robi four times over. In descending order of ages, the grandkids are Dale, Elinor, Brynn, and Silas.

One thing I have learned about being a grampa. It would be good for me if there were a "grandma." She would be the one to gush all over the babies, remember birthdays, buy appropriate presents. I would just tag along and get a bit of the glory for all she has done. My grandkids suffer having a grampa like me. It's a good thing there are some other grandparents!

***

Matt and Breanna are on a Bible-translating journey. I spent a Christmas with them in Juba, South Sudan. I have been to see them a few times in stateside cities. Now they have left for South Asia, to a country I never wanted to return to. I made the long journey to be with them for Christmas 2014, and it was worth the trip.

I would go anywhere to spend time with either of "my boys." They are the apples of my eye. Oh, wouldn't I have longed to feel and hear that I was the apple of my dad's eye? That will never happen, and I have a great felt need to express that to others. Mike and Matt let me do it. You can love someone only to the degree they let you, and they do. It is even more meaningful to me now that my secret has come out. I never wanted to deceive them, but again, I didn't share my secret with anyone. It's another reason I know God loves me. He has given me a relationship with them. There are lots of others where the relationship is very similar. I can't thank God enough for all of them. Just reflecting on all this brings tears to my eyes. I have such a full life. People for me to love and to be loved.

***

Recently, Matt and I were exchanging thoughts on what was the most memorable gift, or important gift, I had given him. At first, he thought it was a wood carving of a lion, with a scroll around its neck, representing Matt's love for God's word and for translating it. I refer to him sometimes as my "Lion King." Then he brought up another memory. I think the following account would be "most memorable" for Mike as well:

In the years I have known these two men, they would talk about going to the mountains of North Carolina. Being someone from California who has backpacked extensively in the Sierra and has spent a lot of time in the Rockies, I would jokingly retort, "Those aren't mountains; they're hills." We would dream about going to see "real mountains" one day. Then they were graduated from college. Then they got married. Then babies started to come. There never was time. Not to mention money. Matt was getting close to beginning his overseas journey.

Suddenly, we saw a window of time, if their wives were agreeable, when we might do it in June of 2011. The ladies agreed. Thank you, Breanna and Mandi! Thankfully, I had lots of frequent-flyer miles, and we left the east coast on a Saturday morning and flew to Reno, Nevada. We rented a car and spent a night with my sister, and then we were off, driving down the eastern side of the Sierra. They saw mountains! BIG mountains. The eastern side of the Sierra is very dramatic. We crossed the Sierra over Sonora Pass and dropped down to the small town of Mariposa where "Mom Aletha" and son, Mark, lived. We went to the Mariposa Grove of sequoias in Yosemite National Park and into Yosemite Valley. There had been a heavy snow-pack that year, and the waterfalls were gushing.

We then went down through the Central Valley of California and over to the San Luis Obispo area, before heading up Highway 1 through Big Sur, looking at elephant seals, exploring Point Lobos, lunching on seafood in Monterey and then up to San Francisco, staying with various friends along the way. We walked on the Golden Gate Bridge, from which we saw Alcatraz. Mike's great desire was to go to Alcatraz. It is called the Rock . . . which is one of my nicknames for Mike because he has grown to be a rock in some men's lives, as well as mine. We also went to the Victorian row houses called the "Painted Ladies," a few blocks from downtown San Francisco. If you don't know what they are, and I did not, then you will have to find out. I thought they had something to do with "ill repute," but they do not. Finally, it was up to Lake Tahoe and then back to Reno. We flew out the following Saturday. What a whirlwind of a trip in one week.

Taking a trip like that allowed me to do something important with the sons I never had. Maybe every dad longs to teach or show his boy some things. I was able to show these sons I never had some of my life and where I grew up. Places that are important to me. The fact that they took the time and saved what money they could to help was a big gift to me. It made me feel that I and my life are important to them. They gave me their time. Quality time is another of my love languages.

That August, for my birthday, Matt made a video of the trip and gave it to me. There are a couple of songs in the video, along with all the pictures, that just swell my heart with joy whenever I watch it. I have made many people endure that video. They have graciously watched it. Thank you all! The video is another of my most treasured possessions.

Chapter Sixteen

Relationships With Women

"Why don't men offer what they have to their women? Because we know down in our guts that it won't be enough."
— John Eldredge, *Wild at Heart*

ALTHOUGH THE SCENE OF MY DAD kissing my unresponsive mom played a role in who or what I am (maybe a very big role), I still made forays into the heterosexual world of men and women.

For starters, like every other boy in America in the mid-1950s, I was in love with Annette Funicello from the "Mickey Mouse Club." I didn't think Spin of "Spin and Marty" fame was bad either. I would go to the TV screen and give Annette a kiss. That was a safe thing to do. I did not, by the way, do the same with Spin.

In the fourth or fifth grade, I went steady for the first time. I had a big heavy ring that I gave to a girl. She wore it around her neck on a chain to show that she was going steady. Looking back, I wonder why she would ever have done that with me. I was this fat kid, not a standout in any way physically or intellectually. We never did anything together. Later, I concluded that she simply needed that ornament to make her more appealing to other guys. It wasn't a positive experience.

In the sixth or seventh grade, I remember being in a movie theater with another girl. I tried to put my arm around her, and she shied away.

Also in junior high, I pursued – slightly – another girl. I even went to Youth for Christ meetings to please her. That, too, went nowhere. The best result of that time was the spiritual seeds that were planted at the YFC meetings.

In high school, there was a girl with whom I had an on-again, off-again relationship. She wasn't physically attractive enough to me, I thought. Not that I was any great catch.

My friends in high school were the type who liked to boast about their conquests. I was a novice in that area, with no experience. I remember trying to "make out" with a girl in the back seat of her brother's car. He was in front with his girl. I had had a lot to drink and was giving it a try. It was all so mechanical. There was no passion, no attraction. I'm sure it must have been awful for her. And for me . . . no thrill at all. That never happened again in my life.

***

Through all of this, I did have the SSA issue. It wasn't overwhelming, and I was content to live my life and keep everyone thinking I was "straight." Even I thought I was, I suppose. That reflected my unwillingness to "go there" and admit who I was. I thought God would get me out of it. At least, I hoped and prayed He would.

It was not until about 1972 that homosexuality was taken off the "mental illness" list. I certainly never saw myself as mentally ill. I am not sure I even knew that information. I just knew it was not a good thing to be.

***

I continued to play the straight role through college. When I came to Christ at age 19, my social circles were not the kind where guys were talking of their conquests, and that was fine with me, especially as long as no one suspected anything about me.

While in college, I worked at a Christian camp in the summer. The camp had a Western theme with cowboy and Indian names used by counselors, and there was one girl who had a hold on me. Her name was "Water Lily." What a great name! If she should read this, she will remember me a bit, I hope. We never did much while at the camp, but we did spend some time together.

After college graduation, I joined Campus Crusade for Christ, and served in the Midwest, a long way from Southern California, where she was. I thought about her a lot and came to a point where I thought she might be the one for me. I prayed for her. In fact, I prayed for her every day. We exchanged letters. I called them "friendship letters." She did reply to them. Then came the time when I went to see her.

My intention was to say that I wanted to enter a more "formal" relationship and see where it would lead. This was a huge step for me. I was excited that I had the courage to do this. Who knew? Maybe this would be what it would take to get me over the "hump."

I can still picture that Sunday afternoon at her apartment. We agreed that I would come over at a certain time, and I did. Eventually, I got around to what I wanted to say. She told me, in her sweet way, how this could not happen. She was engaged and he was to show up soon that day, and he did. I told her how happy I was for her, that at least I had been praying for her all these months as she was coming to the decision to marry him. I cried on the way home. A better word might be sobbed. In those days, the Bee Gees had a popular song: "How Can You Mend a Broken Heart." That was my theme song.

The same scenario happened again years later. I was corresponding with a woman I knew from earlier years. She lived a half a continent away. Over time and correspondence, I came to the same conclusion of wanting to pursue something deeper. When I went to see her . . . she was . . . engaged. Like before, I had been praying for her a lot. My consolation was that she had a lot of prayer cover as she made the choice to marry that man.

Those two experiences helped me to retreat even further into my safe shell and not reach out. I did not like rejection, although I was probably feeling safer. In that way, I didn't have to go deeper into relationships, and I was not at all sure I could deal with one anyway.

***

The older a young single man becomes, if he is serious about his faith, I think the more and more eligible and attractive he becomes to Christian women, especially when he is in his 30s. I was in a singles group in my 30s, and I am very thankful for it. But that was a time when many women (and men) had become single again. Many of those women were looking for someone who was solid in his faith, gave leadership, loved God, and wasn't a total loser in the looks area.

Except for the looks, I fit the bill. Don't get me wrong . . . they weren't knocking my door down. But I was eligible.

I always wanted and hoped I would get married. I kept thinking that, if I can just find the "right one," she will get me over the hump, turn me on, and away we would go. I never had these thoughts in reference to men. The idea of being married to a man, then and now, is not appealing to me. I kept praying to God that He would take this same-sex attraction away. He never did, and I never found the "right one."

I was much more "romantic" (in my mind) with those who were safely far from me. I never had to do anything with them but fantasize. Was I still dealing with my SSA in my private world? Yes.

I used those experiences to explain to questioning people why I was still single. My answer was that I was always afraid to commit. When I did venture out into that world, I only got rejection, which made me even more afraid. Seemed logical enough.

In all those years, I had one recurring nightmare. I would arrive on my wedding day, and on my wedding night be unable to perform. At that point, I would wake up in a sweat. From that time on, I kept a low profile. I did not want to go through rejection again. Nor did I want to deal with those nightmares.

***

During my campus ministry years, when I was in my early 20s, two incidents happened. One concerned a question that I got once in my life. It was from a female co-worker, and we had spent some time together. One time, she outright asked, "Are you gay?" I said no. In all my mental jockeying, I still thought I was not. But I lied to her. I have contacted her since I started this book to ask her forgiveness, which she has graciously given. She is the only one I lied to about this, because she is the only person I can remember ever asking me. I would have told the same lie to others if they had asked.

The question did get me thinking in a more serious way, which led to the other important incident. I asked for, and was allowed, to take a week to go see the psychologist for the ministry I was with. I met with him for five days. In the first session and through my tears, I shamefully shared my story and my fears that I was, in fact, a homosexual. He assured me I was not. He said many men in the ministry came to him with these same fears and tendencies. After a week, he sent me away with that assurance and to "white knuckle" (my phrase) it. He used the 2 Corinthians 10:5 verse: "to take captive every thought and make it obedient to Christ."

I call that "white knuckling" because it is so centered on me and my efforts to keep my thoughts under control. Yes, I have a responsibility, but now I see it as a response to knowing God's love for me. We do have a responsibility to "walk the straight and narrow," so to speak. For me, that responsibility is much more readily accepted and striven for when I am responding to His love for me. At the time, however, I was rejoicing that I was not a homosexual.

So, off I went, determined to take every thought captive. I don't know how long that lasted any more. A week? Maybe five? I fell. When that happened, I moved right back into the life I had been living before and no one knew the better. No one knew why I had gone to see the psychologist, other than for "personal reasons."

***

The next 20 years rolled by. I stayed safe. I dated a little, but always made sure the lady knew this was just a "friendly" thing. I said don't read anything in to it. And it was all fine.

The last time such a scenario happened was in my mid-40s. I had been spending some time with a wonderful lady and always made it clear that we were just doing things as friends. During that time, I got more serious about unreached people groups and missions. Eventually, I left for Indonesia (the details unfold in Chapter Five). After some time there, I began to see what a lonely journey this was going to be. I did not like the prospect of going through it all by myself.

Again, I wrote "the letter" with the safety of 7,000 miles of ocean between us. I did not know when we would be able to see one another, and a relationship by mail seemed good to me. I said perhaps the friendship could grow into something more. I thought, let's see what will happen. She responded positively. Then a new wrinkle appeared.

Unplanned by me, I was home to take a new assignment in the mission. My arrival brought the two of us face to face. Why had I ever written that letter? I knew that, once in the United States again,

I could function fine – alone. I wrote it thinking I was going to be overseas in a lonely setting, and I didn't want to be alone. She was a wonderful lady, and if I ever was going to have a partner, there was no one else I would want. Not that I was worthy of her. I was not.

Then I put so much pressure on us. I had about six weeks to raise additional financial support. I was determined to leave Fresno either engaged or in no relationship at all. She often said to not put such pressure on myself. She knew my hesitancies, although not the reason for them. By the time I left Fresno, nothing had been resolved.

When I was safely 4,000 miles away, I broke it off in a telephone conversation. Later, I found out that day was her birthday. I resolved I would never do that again to anyone – or mislead any other woman again, only to back out, which I seemingly always did. Yes, there were some situations where the lady was already engaged, but I would have backed out at some point even in those relationships. It was obvious who I was and I could not escape it. I had a full and productive life, for which I was (and am) thankful, and I would simply continue on in that single life.

***

I still think of having a female partner. Looking back, I wish there might have been a way to share my SSA with a woman and have her accept the reality that our marriage would not be consummated. Even if I found such a partner, I don't think she could tolerate living with me. I am very content with where I am. But I do long for relationship, as do we all.

Someone asked me what it was like to achieve non-sexual intimacy. An interesting question. I am not sure one ever "achieves" intimacy. It would seem that you can only be as intimate as your last honest conversation and understanding. As soon as some deception sneaks in, then your intimacy starts to wane. Having my darkest secret come out has given me the opportunity to be as open, and intimate, as I ever could be. The intimacy I think I have found with people, even the closest people to me, is still not what one could have in marriage. I am thankful for what I have, although it does not totally eliminate times of loneliness.

Gregory Martin quotes his father in his book, *"Stories for Boys."* In it, his dad is quoted as saying, "I did hide behind a huge mask of pretense, just to have what I felt would be a normal life. As it turns out, I never had a normal life without pretense and a false front . . . . " That is me. I can easily justify myself by saying, "We all do that to some degree." The fact remains, I had a false front. Now, I do not.

Chapter Seventeen

To Whom Can I Go?

"Instead, speaking the truth in love, we will grow to become in every respect the mature body of him who is the head, that is, Christ."

— Ephesians 4:15

I WROTE ABOUT CONVERGENCE EARLIER. Little did I know that the most significant part of my life was going to come out and converge with the rest.

In my time here on the deck, I have found a refreshing – though threatening – honesty in the young men who come my way. They talk about things that my generation usually avoids religiously. They talk very openly, for example, about masturbation. I remember very well the first man who came to me with the issue, which often is coupled with Internet pornography.

Here he was, so frustrated with himself, seemingly looking to me for answers or help. I cannot remember ever having such a conversation before – not in my Christian journey of 40 years at that point. Nobody went there.

I fumbled with a response, wondering whether he ever considered why he would do that, what he was searching for, and to not judge himself too harshly. I never admitted having the same struggle. I portrayed myself as being too old for that issue anymore, and guys usually never asked me. However, they were open with their struggles. Little did they know it does not go away in older men, as much as we pretend otherwise.

Why do I share that story? Because it is the same story for our men (and women) whom churches and mission agencies send overseas to "reach the world." We put these people on pedestals sometimes. We think they are spiritual giants many times when, in fact, they are dealing with the same issues we are. The difference is, they are in strange and isolated places.

In my years in Member Care, I either helped others with, or heard about, such issues as depression . . . suicide . . . pornography and masturbation . . . unfaithfulness . . . SSA . . . and on and on. It seems to me that possibly the biggest hindrance in beginning to deal with our seemingly insurmountable problems is that there is no one to talk to. At least we don't think there is – and certainly not anyone who is safe and who would understand, and who would not tell our leaders or a sending church.

***

On the foreign field, I made a good friend who was a highly effective missionary, having led several people to Christ. He was married with kids. It came out that he had same-sex attraction. He was with another mission agency, not the one I was with. In the end, he had to leave the mission field and return home. In the times I was able to be with him, I was empathetic and caring, but I never shared my issue. I simply did not go there with anyone, even someone like him, who obviously would have been supportive.

After my crash and the truth was out, I made it a point to go see him and his wife. Thankfully, they remain married and their kids are doing great. I needed to share my story with them and ask their forgiveness for not doing so earlier and for not "being there for them" as I could have been. Thankfully, they have forgiven me, and I feel close to him although I rarely see them. It is one more example of what is "out there" and we have no clue. I think there are a good deal more struggles with SSA, whether in the missionary community or merely at church, than we want to think.

***

I have heard that the accepted number is at least 50 percent of missionaries, especially men, but not exclusively, look at pornography. My guess is, it is more. Now, what are they to do with that? If I go to my colleague, he may tell the team leader. If I go to the team leader, he may tell the area leader who may contact the Member Care office. I, the afflicted missionary, am petrified that the mission agency will send me home and, when my sending church finds out, the church's leaders will bring me home. It's a double whammy and all very shameful. In general, I am sure there is no real safety on the field. So we missionaries do not share our struggles. Or we wait until it is too late. We get caught or something disastrous happens. Again, the overall understanding, unspoken of course, is "don't ask . . . don't tell." Or, if asked . . . lie.

What would my ideal policy be? A hard question, as I don't think there can be a black-and-white policy. The atmosphere needs to be one of risky acceptance, in which people feel free to share their issues without the fear of what will happen to them, or be imposed upon them. A person cannot simply join an organization and find more grace than what is normal in the overall Christian world. So this cannot be resolved by one mission agency deciding how it is going to be. We all come to an agency with baggage and, even though the agency may say it is governed by grace, we won't believe it if all our experiences are otherwise.

Believe it or not, the people with all these issues, and I am one of them, love God just as much as you. They want to serve Him. They have a real desire to do what they are doing. They simply have these issues, and the issues sometimes get exacerbated because they are alone. They feel powerless in this new culture. They have no friends or anyone else with whom to talk. At the same time, they think they are supposed to be spiritual giants, able to deal singlehandedly with their shameful, insurmountable struggles. When all comes to light, they generally are brought back to the States for "restoration." Some may find their way back to the field, but many do not.

***

The idea of "restoration" is one that puzzles me. When my secret came out and I went to the counseling center for three months, I learned at the end that my job was over. One suggestion was that I might work as an intern at my church for a year for the purpose of being restored. I could continue to receive support from donors through the mission agency. Almost everyone liked that idea, even my sending church. Everyone was fighting for me, and I am so thankful. But there were no guarantees that I would be allowed to return to the Member Care team or take a new mission job – even if I had a good report of restoration. I declined the offer.

I wondered, "What does it look like to be 'restored'?" The truth about me had come out. I was dealing with it. Why did I need restoration any more than anyone else? I had faithful donors who believed in me, no matter what I did or where I went. I could not ask them to keep giving to something that I did not necessarily agree with.

Does restoration mean that I don't act out any more? That I read my Bible daily for some strict or prescribed amount of time? That I am no longer tempted? That I appear like whatever a "restored" person supposedly does and looks like? That I love God in some more evident way than I already do?

In John 21:15-25, the Apostle Peter seems to have been restored by Jesus soon after his sins of denial. Huge denial, it seems to me. How would we "restore" a person who had denied Jesus in such a public way, especially if he were a leader in the church? How would we "restore" King David these days in the church? He was guilty of fantasizing, adultery, lying, murder. How would we deal with that restoration? And what would be the process? He wrote some psalms of regret and repentance. I love Psalm 51. How many times have I read that over the years, especially when I think I have been excessively sinful? We read that and think that David has been restored. I will stop here. I fear I am offending a lot of readers.

As I say in an earlier chapter, I am the offending one. I am looking for grace and acceptance. The offended ones are thinking they have offered more than enough grace. Somewhere in the middle is the common ground, but both parties have to be willing to go to the middle.

Now I grant you that, for married people and breaches of trust, it is more complicated. But I do ponder how one is restored after a fall, and what does that look like? And who should be deciding that? Some would say "the church." I am not saying the church should not. I simply wonder about all this.

***

Although discussed earlier, I will risk bringing it up again. Another issue for men, missionary or not, is the idea of being the "apple of your father's eye." Consider that the conversation and question go like this: "I am not asking if your father loved you as you grew up. I presume you will tell me he did. BUT, as you grew up, did you feel as if you were the apple of your father's eye?" Again, around 80 percent answer no. I answer no. I did not think my father was proud of me. Even when I accomplished something, I did not feel that way.

I have Christian brothers who are fathers and say much the same. "How can I be proud of my son if he has done nothing to be proud of?" Maybe you are a father of young boys and would say the same thing. So, how are we to live a missionary life, or otherwise, when we are not even sure of His love for us or that we are His beloved sons? Oh, you can do it. After all, John 3:16 tells me that God so loved the world. That includes me. It is usually that kind of love that we are imparting as we labor. Head knowledge, but not a heartfelt knowledge. It's the difference between your father putting food on the table and clothes on your back, because he loves you. But you never feel as if you are the apple of his eye or that he is proud of you simply because you are his son. It's better than nothing, but not helpful for those who want to know the real joy of the Lord. As you can see, knowing your earthly father's possessive love for you will affect knowing your heavenly Father's love.

It has been helpful to me over these last years to dwell on certain parables. The prodigal father and wayward son. Luke 15:11-32. So familiar, but realizing what love that father had for his son. I know it is generally referred to as the parable of the Prodigal Son, but in recent years I have read books referring to the Prodigal Father. It seems the title given to it is a misnomer. Actually, it is the father who acted so prodigiously, or lavishly, not the son. Although the son did lavishly squander his money. Or, when Jesus is baptized and the voice comes saying, "This is my Son, whom I love; with him I am well pleased." Matthew 3:17. Brennan Manning writes about how Jesus, in His humanity, needed to hear this. As do we. Another is when John lays his head on Jesus' chest in John 21:20. He is at that point hearing the very heartbeat of God. Can you imagine doing that? Leaning back and looking into His eyes. Seeing His love for you. Hearing His heartbeat. All those passages have been very helpful to me to experience God's love for me in a personal way.

Another question I might ask is, "What do you think of when you hear the word, 'love'?" Most all answers are geared to how WE are not as loving as WE should be . . . towards wives, kids, others. Only once did I get this answer: "God. I think of how much God loves me." When I mention that lone response, someone may say, "Oh, yeah. Well, that is for sure." But it is not what they think of immediately. Most of us don't, I'd venture to say. When we think of love, we think of how well we are, or are not, doing in this area. In *"The Shack,"* author William P. Young calls it "living loved." If you are not living loved, then you are like a bird with his wings clipped. You cannot fly as God intended you to.

Thus, the biggest issues on the field or in the local church are that we do not feel safe and secure in the love of others or sometimes even in the arms of God. On the field, we live in more fear than ever, so far away from all our normal support systems. Where is the love and care?

Chapter Eighteen

God Is Good

"God is good . . . all the time. All the time . . . God is good."

H OW MANY TIMES HAVE I been in gatherings of Christian people when that chant went out?

How many times have I read or heard prayer requests regarding an urgent crisis? They are mostly about health, but also financial or personal needs. Spots were found . . . please pray that the biopsy comes back clear. I will be traveling . . . pray for journey mercies. You know what I mean. Sometime later, word comes from that person. All is benign, crisis resolved . . . God is good. The money came in . . . God is good.

That is when I wonder why I rarely hear, "The tumor is malignant . . . God is good." "My unwed daughter is pregnant . . . God is good." "My son has just come out of the closet . . . God is good." I am not saying you will hear it from me either, as much as I would like to be that kind of person. You will hear "praise the Lord" as the first thing out of my mouth. Decades ago, it seemed better than "aw, sh— ." People know I say "praise the Lord," and I think it helps me to keep a better perspective on things.

I said it when, a year apart, my Dad and then Mom died. My sister was with me both times, and she said, if I remember correctly, that she was surprised at first and then thankful to hear me say that. It was a loving, yet strong thing to say as we walked into my dad's hospital room to find the bed we left him in the night before was being made up for someone else. When the attending nurse asked us who we were and we said that we are the children of the man who was in the bed last night, she seemed surprised and said, "Don't you know?"

"Know what?"

"He passed away last night."

"Praise the Lord."

When my sister and I walked into the room where my mother was, dying of cancer, and where I had been just a few hours before, we saw Mom lying in the bed with the oxygen tube across her chest and not in her nose. I saw something was wrong, grabbed my sister around the shoulders and led her out, stopping at the front desk to say something is wrong in our mother's bedroom. There was a flurry of activity, and then we were told Mom had died and they did not know it. Praise the Lord.

***

In 2006, as I embarked on this wonderful life on the deck, I was learning and believing more and more how I was truly God's beloved son. I was the apple of His eye. I loved it so much. Then I had an opportunity to test my new confidence that His heart toward me was good.

As I have said, I have been totally deaf in my left ear my whole life. Most people didn't know because I heard very well with my right ear.

Over 60-plus years, I never did lose my hearing. I did quite well until about 2009. I woke up one morning, and I could tell something had happened. It was not gradual. Once it did happen, it seemed to be getting gradually worse. I was going to an ear, nose, and throat doctor, and it seemed I was going deaf in front of his eyes and he was doing nothing about it.

It was later that I sat on the deck and asked myself whether I really believed God's heart toward me was good. If I were to go deaf, would that be coming out of the goodness of His heart? I wrestled with that and concluded that, even though I may see no good in it, I would be able to look back and see how it was a good thing. Therefore, it was a good thing. It came from His heart of good toward me.

I don't hear so well anymore. I don't hear certain tonal ranges. Music is not appealing to me, except for all the old songs that are programed in my brain. As the Doobie Brothers sang, *"Music is the doctor...."* For me, it has been and still is. Old music that I still know.

People have to repeat a lot. I don't go to noisy places as it hurts my ear. I stick to the deck mostly, where I can hear relatively well. Even as I write this and want to say, "God is good," I feel like a hypocrite because I have a good life. I think I would say it even if I lost all my hearing today.

I never thought my life, post-crash, would turn out good. However, today I am loved, I have some gainful part-time employment, people come to the deck in all the numbers I can handle, even with my secret for all to see. Yes . . . God is good. What if it were the opposite? I trust I would still say, these days, God is good. Or, at least, praise the Lord.

When my secret first came out, did I default to "God is good?" No. God is there, but right now not good. As I say above, friends know that I am quick to say "praise the Lord" in tough situations. I do think that, as I walked out of the pastor's office, my attitude was more like that than the opposite. It still did not keep me from wanting the return flight I was on to go down.

We are so quick to determine what is good and what is not. We may deny it, but many of us really think we know better than God what is best for us and others. I think of *"The Shack"* again, as it has some thought-provoking reading material. God says, at one point, "I understand how difficult it is for you [humans], so lost in your perceptions of reality and yet so sure of your own judgments. . . . " I really like that line. Later, God says, "You have such a small view of what it means to be human." How do YOU determine what is good or not? Think about it.

***

Loneliness. I have been re-reading a good book that deals with SSA. *Washed and Waiting* by Wesley Hill. He talks about the loneliness that homosexual Christians deal with. I must say I also like the way he refers to people like us. We are Christians. We are God's people. We are not "homosexuals." That makes it a noun, and he likes that word to be an adjective. He can more readily use "gay Christians," or the like. As I said earlier, the word "gay," and even "homosexual," indicates lifestyle, to me. Thus, I like the term SSA. For sure, it's all semantics, but as I am new to all this openness, that is where I come down.

As Hill talks about loneliness, I pondered it. There have been times when I have been lonely. Loneliness is not something unique to SSA people. I also know there are times when married people are lonely. Marriage is not all deep affirmation and talk. It is true of all single people to one degree or another.

From an early point in my adult life, I have actively avoided loneliness. If I saw a Friday or Saturday looming ahead, with nothing on the calendar to do, I often would call someone to say, "Can I come over that night? I'd be happy to bring the steaks." If they were free, they usually said yes, and we had a good time. Yes, one can be surrounded by people but still feel lonely. I am sure there have been times like that for me. At least I have tried to avoid being alone too much. Nevertheless, I have grown to like being alone when the end of the evening comes, especially if an event has been at my place. I like doing dishes and reflecting on a great evening. I like it when I see and know that people have enjoyed themselves – when there has been good conversation, deep sharing, and prayer.

The real loneliness comes when you think you have no one to share your deepest issues with. I had chosen that route, wanting to keep my secret hidden. Because I did, I did not have anyone until a few years ago. Now, I have everyone. Hallelujah!

Wesley Hill refers to the idea that SSA people think they are perpetually, hopelessly unsatisfying to God. I agree for the most part. I felt that way most of my adult Christian life, until 2007 (after I moved to the deck) when I started to more deeply understand and accept His unconditional love for me. Not His pity, but His love. I feel secure in knowing I am His beloved son. I don't feel unsatisfying to God. I feel wanted, pursued, secure, approved, safe. My regenerate heart is a good thing . . . not a deceitful and wicked thing.

***

My biggest fear relates to future loneliness. I fear getting older, fear having some terminal disease that incapacitates me and not having family to take me in. Many have said, "We will, Rob." They say they want to, but do they, when reality arrives along with a hospital bed in their house and me in it? They will have to feed me, bathe me, take care of me. That is hard. Without being blood relatives, I fear that it is too much to ask of anyone. I also fear being stuck in a convalescent hospital that smells of urine, and I don't have the money to be in a better place. When I start having those thoughts, I need to remember that "God is good." I need to get out of living in a fearful, godless future and get back to the present, where God is.

***

Even in the present, I still have a struggle. I want to be this towering rock of strength, stability, love, and self-control. A paragon of biblical virtue. To whom? To all those with whom I meet. To those whom I have discipled or mentored. Despite their insistence of respect and love for me, I think that I have let them down. I have failed them. I am not who they thought I was and therefore I am not good. I know it isn't true. I would much rather wrestle with this now that the total truth is known about me than before, when no one knew who I REALLY was. This applies only to those who knew me "pre-crash." Those who have gotten to know me since don't have that false illusion about me.

In it all, God is good.

***

I recently was asked whether I regretted my life. A resounding "NO!" came out. Oh, I have mixed emotions at times. They are all the "why me's?" that people go through. It would have been nice to have a family. To have had a wife that had eyes for only me. Kids ... arrows in my quiver ... that I was shooting out to impact the world. But I often think that my life has been far better this way. I think that my SSA has given me more time to become a better discipler and mentor than I ever would have been if I were otherwise.

What does the Apostle Paul say about this? Among other things, he wished many of us could be like him in his singleness. 1 Cor. 7:32-34. An unmarried man can be more concerned about the Lord's affairs. I have been able to do that.

Mine was a very safe world to operate in, with no pressure. Did I get a lot of fulfillment and meaning out of it? For sure. Having no family, these were and are the "family" that Jesus talks about having many times over. My former colleagues at the mission agency wondered, I am sure, whether my ministry with men on the deck was "healthy." Not that they feared anything physical was going on, but what was really going on my in head? And maybe heart? They had reason for that, I think. I had admitted my SSA. The men were young. I spent a lot of time with them. I did see myself as an older brother figure to some and maybe even father figure in some ways to some. I did like that. Is that unhealthy? Healthy? I don't know.

I think I have affected far more people for the Kingdom than I would have had I lived a "normal" life. I am thankful for that. Numbers are not important. But they are there. I have all the time in the world to invest in other people. And I do it. I love it. I need it.

As I age, I don't mind having a free evening to be here on the deck by myself. Sip some scotch. Watch the cardinals and other birds. Think. Pray. Cogitate. By 7 o'clock, I used to feel a bit antsy, wishing someone would come over. Not now. I average seeing at least five guys a week in the evenings, sometimes more. There are some morning times with different ones. I don't think I could do all that if I were married. I am thankful and I would not have it any other way. Really. I don't see myself anymore as damaged goods and disappointing to God. I am His boy! When He thinks of me, His heart swells with joy. He is quite fond of me. And that is not because of what I do. It is because of who I am. The apple of His eye.

Regrets? NO!

God is good.

Footprints in the Snow

S O T H E R E Y O U H A V E I T. In the Preface, I refer to myself as having been the HMOE. The Happiest Man on Earth. Then came the crash, and all that happened as a result of that.

Several months ago, the man who had given me that label was here. I was sharing with him all that had transpired since the crash and how that God, in His mercy, had restored all the deck-life I had before, but in an even better way. The openness and honesty are better than before, because I am even more open and honest. I was before, but not totally. Now, nobody leaves the deck not knowing the essentials of my story. How many times have I heard a comment something like this, "Well, Rob, because you have been so honest with me, let me share something with you that I have never shared."

John said, "Sounds to me, Rob, like the HMOE is back." As I thought about it I decided that was not quite true anymore. Now, I think I am the TMOE. The Thankfullest Man on Earth. I know "thankfullest" is not a word, but it is to me, and it fits the HMOE model.

During the crash and soon thereafter, I could never have imagined that I would have the life I now live. Although I wish I never had to go through all this, it has been the best thing for me. I am so thankful. God does redeem our messed up lives if we will let Him, not that I made a choice to let Him do so. I was found out, shamed, kicking and screaming all the way through the birth canal into my new life. I did not want to go there. But now that I am there . . . I am glad I am. And thankful.

During the writing of this book, I have felt like a miner, panning the streams of his memory. Thanks for that metaphor goes to Brennan Manning. There are a lot of gold nuggets in my stream and some that I have not yet found. I am thankful for all of them.

***

Recently, I shared my story in front of the congregation at my church. There are those who wonder why I wanted or needed to go there and do that. Writing this book might be included in that. My response is that I want to redeem my story and help stimulate the church into a more open, honest, and safe discussion of these matters. A friend said that he thought this is already a wide-open discussion in the church. My only response is that I don't think so. Not in my experience. Maybe it is among the younger generation, but there are still a lot of us older generation people who do not want to go there. We don't understand it, and we don't really want to. I am not talking about blogs and books that do deal with this. Maybe, in that sense, there IS a lot of discussion in the church.

I'm talking about the person next to me or you in the pew. The people you fellowship with each Sunday, and where I can't say things anonymously (as I can in a blog). I need to be more guarded. Or, at least I think I do.

The response from my church was great. Several people I don't even know came up to say something like, "This is so needed. YOU are so needed."

***

I am not advocating or approving of same-sex marriage, or even sexual activity. I am not in favor of it. Someone said we had "already lost the battle" for gay marriage. I thought, why is it always a battle that we must win or lose? This "us against them" mentality. I wonder what it would look like if we had "won" that battle? Do we settle back in our chairs and think all is right with the world, now that we have won? Do we look for another battle to win? Is that what the Christian life is all about?

Do you think that people with SSA somehow love God less than you? Do they desire to serve God less than you? Are they are less qualified to serve God than you? Really, do you somehow think they are second-class citizens? Most of us would say "no." But what does your life say? What do your words and thoughts that no one hears say? Up to the time when my story came out, I would guess that most thought I was a very dedicated Christian. That I had walked the "road less traveled." I gave up a chance for a very well-off life in real estate had I not chosen the missionary route. People would have entrusted their children to me, their young men. Although they may still do these things, I think there will be some hesitancy within them, especially if they did not know me or my history.

I have no idea what the statistics show, but I would guess that, in general, people think that someone identified with SSA is a danger to society, more so than heterosexual people. I don't think so. Statistics most likely would show that it is about equal. But I think the perception is not that way. Someone molests a child. It comes out that they are of the SSA type. The spoken or unspoken word is, "I thought so."

I don't have answers for these questions. I just want to help stimulate discussion in a healthy manner. I don't want to win battles; I just want to relate and discuss and help those with deep secrets so they can have a safe place to share them and maybe even deal with them. The church should be that place. Not always a counselor's office.

***

I have enjoyed reading "*The Shack*" by William Paul Young. And then re-reading, and re-reading all my underlined parts. It has so many great ideas that challenge me. One is to live in the present. Maybe I am more affected by the truth that I live too much in the future, where God is rarely present, and it is mostly through a lens of fear. As Young says, it isn't even real. While I try to set up everything just right so I won't have to be afraid of growing old or needing someone's help, as I described earlier. Fear and trust cannot co-exist. We try to couch or cover our fears with "being responsible." Not good. Being responsible is OK. I am responsible, I hope. But I trust you get my drift.

Another is the idea of redemption. In "*The Shack*," when the question is brought up to God as to how He can justify the death of Mack's child, God interrupts to say that He is not justifying it; He wants to redeem it. When I read that, I realized I needed to do the same. I cannot justify who I am or what I have done with it. I want to redeem it. I see this book as part of that process.

***

I am sure some readers might conclude that I am advocating something. Others will think I am not advocating anything and shame on me. Either way, I might be seen as one more voice in the winning or losing of the battle. To some, I might be the "good guy." To others, the "bad guy." Or maybe that I am "not responsible" in thinking this through. Or not scriptural. Whatever their agenda might be. Having an agenda is not bad, I don't think. I have one, too.

Am I saying, "God created me this way?" I get lots of push-back from that kind of statement. Some of it my own. But how DID I get here? Did I make some conscious choice way back when? I don't think so. If I could have made the choice to escape it, I would have. Is it a mix of the "nature/nurture" idea? I don't know. I see plenty of men who had far worse father-son relationships than I, and that did not move them to SSA. I see others who did have a great parental relationship, and they did move to SSA. How do I reconcile the fact that God knit me together in my mother's womb? That He created my inmost being? That all the days ordained for me were written in His book before one of them came to be? All those ideas are contained in Psalm 139.

I think this is the life He ordained for me. I think I am the man, His beloved son, that He wants me to be. I think He wants to redeem my story and to bring Him honor and joy. That's what I think and what I want to do. I have read many times the idea that our greatest gifts come from our greatest wounds. I think that is probably true, and I hope it is true for me. Some might say, "You are not wounded; you are just suffering the consequences of your sin." Maybe so. But I think that all that has been revealed about me was the biggest wound I could ever have and live with.

I don't want to be in anybody's face, saying, "This is who I am, so deal with it." I am not saying, "This is who I am and you can be, too. It's OK."

I am just saying this is who I am . . . fallen, redeemed, loved.

Recently, I read Walt Harrington's book "*The Everlasting Stream.*" In it, he quotes his father who said: "Everything's beautiful if you look at it right." My life is beautiful. Your life is beautiful . . . if we look at it right . . . especially as followers of Christ. As the saying, or song goes, "God don't make no junk." (The Halo Benders) Because I believe that is true, I hope we, as the community of Christ, will find a new willingness and openness to share our deepest secrets with one another. Or, if we are not the one sharing, then we can be the safe person who is listening without judging.

A friend said I should have a chapter titled, "Footprints in the Snow." He was thinking that, as new, deep snow has fallen, someone has to go out and make the first footprints that others can follow in. I am certainly not the first person to write about SSA issues. But I hope my "footprints" will create a path that others can walk on and build on as well, knowing someone has gone before.

My Message to My Church Family

I READ THE FOLLOWING TO MY church family at Orlando Grace Church on Aug. 3, 2014. The request I ask of them, I ask of you!

I want to thank my God and Heavenly Father for His grace and mercy to me. And I thank the elders for allowing me to share a bit of my life story with you.

Some of you may remember when, about two years ago, I left Orlando for several months. I said that I was taking some time off to deal with some personal issues, which I was. But it has only been within the last year that I have arrived at a place where I have become more open with what that issue was and is. And that is what I want to share with you, my church family, now.

Two years ago, I admitted for the first time in my life that I had a struggle with Same-Sex Attraction (SSA). It is a secret I have kept all my life for fear of the consequences that would happen to me if I ever shared it. But in keeping my secret, I have been deceitful to everyone I have known. I have not trusted God to be there for me. For this, I have asked God, and now I ask you, for forgiveness.

Please know that I have never acted on this with another person. Nor have I ever wanted to. Although that does not mean that I have not had an ongoing struggle with thought life and the like. I have. And do.

I have always feared that, if I ever revealed my secret, I would suffer many consequences. All negative. One of which would be the loss of all my friends. I have learned that I was very wrong there. I have been loved and accepted. Not judged.

I have had a lot of time to ponder what "grace" means. I have experienced what I think is real grace here at OGC. Grace, to me, now means, among other things, risky acceptance. That has happened here. I have offered to step down from various responsibilities, and those who would decide have said no. They wanted me to stay. I am so thankful.

I have three major reasons for sharing this today. One is that I want to be fully known. We have heard sermons in the last months challenging us to be vulnerable with one another and to be known. That if we are 99 percent known and 1 percent unknown, then we are not known. That does not mean that we should all be up here, doing what I am doing now. I have made myself known to many in this last year. But I would like to be known within my church family at large.

The second reason is to give courage to all of us to be known. We probably all have secrets that we do not want anyone to know. Your issue may be similar to mine, or something totally different. But whatever it is, you probably think it is the worst thing in the world, and no one could have a bigger problem than yours. I certainly felt that way. Can I say that we are sinning against God and one another when we do not allow others to bear our burdens with us?

The third reason is redemption. I read a book in the last year in which the main character has lost his young daughter to kidnapping and death. He is having a conversation with God and starts to say something like: " . . . how can you justify . . . " when God interrupts and says, "Mack, I am not justifying it, I am redeeming it." And that is what I desire to do with the days I have left. Redeem my life journey and who I am. This is one step in this redemptive journey.

I have come to know God's deep love for me over these last eight years. Truly believing I am His beloved son. That I am the apple of His eye. Had I not, I don't know how I would have made it through this.

But I am now pressing on. I am free. I am forgiven. My deepest, darkest secret is in the light. Many of you know that over the years I have had a sort of mentoring role with men on my deck by the lake.

Those have been great times. But now they are even better because I have become fully honest. This has only made the deck a safer and more honest and accepting place. This is another aspect of redemption. There are others.

I thank God for His forgiveness of me, and, once again, I ask for yours. I am available and wanting to discuss this with anyone who hears or reads these words.

Thank you.

If anyone wants to interact with me on this, go to my Website, *www.decktherapy.com*. I would love to hear from you!

Rob

Deck Therapy Questions

Good ones to always start with:

1. What makes you mad? What else?

2. What makes you sad? What else?

3. What makes you glad? What else?

4. What are you afraid of these days? What else?

5. Are you consumed by your marriage? Purity? Then why are you so consumed with pornography or masturbation?

6. What is more important to God (and you), your knowledge or your character?

7. Do you cherish your wife? Do you feel cherished?

8. Do you want your son to grow up and be just like you? Why or why not?

True Faced by Bill Thrall, Bruce McNicol, and John Lynch

1. Do you see yourself as Godly, or valiantly trying to become godly? (Page 60)

2. When people ask you how you are, what do you say? Fine?

3. What is the most revealing commentary of your theology? Answer: How you view yourself. (65)

4. Do you influence others more out of what you do or who you are? (74)

5. Does knowing you make people better? (76)

6. To what degree can people love you? Answer: To the degree you let them. (90)

Wild at Heart by John Eldredge

- When hard things happen, what is your question of God? Why are you doing this to me, or what are you trying to teach me? (105)

The Way of the Wild Heart by John Eldredge

1. What is the greatest gift your father gave you? It is always the passing on of masculinity. (5)

2. What is a most treasured memory of your father?

3. Does your life show that you value more service FOR or intimacy WITH God? (13)

4. Agree or disagree: "When we look at our fathers, we fear that they are what we are and what we will become." (28)

5. "Forgiveness was made available to each of us SO THAT we might come home to the Father. Forgiveness is NOT the goal. COMING HOME to the Father is the goal. " (30)

6. Did you feel safe with your father? (42)

7. Did you feel you were the apple of his eye? (42)

8. How would YOU love to be fathered these days? (61)

9. Where did you feel missed as a boy? (70)

10. When have you felt triumphant? (105)

Genesis 3

1. Where are you?

2. How do you hide from God?

3. Who told you?

4. What is this you have done? Not a crime like theft, but a betrayal of love.

The Sacred Romance by Brent Curtis and John Eldredge

1. In your outer life, do you live from "ought or desire?" (6)

2. What better describes your spiritual journey? Communion with God or activity for God? (6)

3. "Each of us has a geography where the Romance first spoke to us. It is usually the place we both long to see again and fear returning to for fear our memories will be stolen from us." (14)

4. What were "arrows" for you as you grew up? (24) What have they tempted you to do? (27)

5. "Connection with mother and father, so necessary to living with courage and hope." (24)

6. What creates a sense of "wonderment" in you? (31)

7. What have the arrows you have known tempted you to do? (27)

8. What did you dream of doing as a child? (44) Favorite fairy tale? (44)

9. Should we live with hopeful abandon, trusting in a larger story whose ending is good, or should we live in our small stories and glean what we can from the Romance while trying to avoid the arrows? (47)

10. Compare God's goodness to safety. (57)

11. Is the fall of Adam and Eve a crime like theft or a betrayal of love? (78)

12. Who is the hero in scripture? It is only in seeing Him as the hero of the larger story that we come to know His heart is good. (82)

13. Most people live with a subtle dread that one day they will be discovered for who they really are and the world will be appalled. Agree/disagree. (84)

14. Have you ever been wanted for your heart, your truest self? 91

15. What do you need in order to love God with all your heart? Living with total freedom. (107)

16. Can you ever satisfy God's law without killing your heart and earning your keep? Do you think God really loves you beyond your usefulness? (109)

17. Jesus invites us to thirst. Satan invites us to control through performance of one kind or another. Agree/disagree. (113)

18. Is your story powerful enough to sustain your waning years? (115)

19. Do people marry for safety or emotional intimacy? (118)

20. "The Haunting." What is your life song? (123)

21. Pretending that life is easier and more blessed than it really is hinders our ability to walk with God and share him with others. Faith is not the same thing as denial. Agree/disagree. (150)

22. What is the ruling sentence of your heart? (154) "What I feared has come upon me."

23. "Faith looks back and draws courage. Hope looks ahead and keeps desire alive." (158)

24. Are your prayers more of the "do this" and "do that" variety? Do you think you have communed with God? (164)

25. Is your spiritual journey a "love affair" or a burdensome, heavy, exhausting journey? (165)

26. Are you abiding in Jesus? If not, then where is it that you do abide? (165)

27. Do you want to be or think that you are someone's hero? (168)

28. Do you think of spiritual progress as requiring you to do more? (168)

29. Faith, hope, love. Which is most important to you? Love is the greatest, but hope plays the deciding role. Faith and love depend on hope (Col. 1:5). (178)

30. Do you live as if this life is your ONLY hope? (179)

31. What is the strongest enemy of faith? Dullness, not doubt. Of love? Indifference, not hate. (181)

32. What would you like your new name to be, given to us on a white stone? (Rev. 2:17) (183)

Surrender to Love by David Benner

1. What do you long for, or what is the deepest ache of your soul? Connection and belonging. (12)

2. Do you focus more on obedience or surrender? (10)

3. What do you assume God thinks when you come to mind? (15)

4. What is the focus in the prodigal son parable? The prodigality of the father . . . not the misdeeds of the son. (19)

5. What "settles you in God?" (19)

6. Were we created for worship or friendship with God? (23)

7. What do you know about God from direct personal experience, as opposed to belief? (27)

8. Do you call yourself a Christian based more on belief or experience? (27) "Knowledge by acquaintance is always better than mere knowledge by description." A.W. Tozer

9. If God is love, can he be known objectively? No. He cannot be known apart from love. (28)

10. Have you accepted ideas about God as substitutes for direct experience of him? (28)

11. Do you believe in God or know God? (28) Carl Jung

12. Do you consider yourself to be more rational or emotional? Does how you answer that determine how you approach God? (30)

13. Are you more rational or emotional? Does your answer determine how, therefore, you know God? (31) "The deepest need for all human beings is to surrender to Perfect Love."

14. Is your God one who requires appeasement in some way? (35)

15. Do you fear that for which you most deeply long? (32)

16. Is your obedience out of duty or surrender? (36)

17. Do you love your fear and fear the loss that would be involved in giving fear up? (36)

18. Is fear the enemy, or is it a spiritual virtue? (37)

19. Do you resist unconditional love . . . Perfect Love? Most do because it demands surrender. (46)

20. Does God want us to feel afraid of Him? (47)

21. If God were sitting in front of you and looking into your eyes, what would you say? What would He say? (48)

22. What is our substitute for surrender? Obedience. (55)

23. What is involved in repentance? Turning from or to? (74)

24. The more you fear, the less you know love. Where are you on the scale? (83)

25. Do you want a spirituality of improvement or transformation? (91)

26. Do you function more from a "me" or "we" mentality? (93)

27. What causes genuine transformation in us? Allowing ourselves to be loved unconditionally. (96)

28. Is love something we "do" or something we are? (97)

29. What casts out fear? Knowing love or Perfect Love. (79) The more I fear, the less I know love (me).

The Gift of Being Yourself by **David Benner**

1. As we become more like Christ, do we become more like each other? (16)

2. Whom do you pretend to be? (15)

3. What is the most important thing for you existence and well-being? Knowing yourself. (19)

4. Is it important to know yourself in your knowing of God? (20)

5. What do you value more, knowledge or love? (23)

6. You may not tell lies, but do you live them? (24)

7. What is worth more, a little knowledge OF God, or a great deal of knowledge ABOUT God? (35)

8. What have you learned about yourself as a result of your experience with God? And what do you know about God as a result of genuine encounter with yourself? (30)

9. Because God is love,God can only be known through love. (35)

10. The Christian God is known ONLY in devotion, not objective detachment. (35)

11. Is your relationship with God based more on what you believe or on what you experience? (39)

12. Most of us learn to discern God's presence by first looking for it in the rearview mirror. (43)

13. Is your identity based on what you do or who you are? (50)

14. The God who is Divine community is known only in human community. No one should ever expect to make the journey alone. (52)

15. Is your Christian identity based on being a sinner or a deeply loved sinner? (64)

16. Did you grow up believing that if you were a good boy, you would earn love? (85)

17. Where do your deep gladness and the world's deep hunger meet? That is the place God calls you to. (97)

18. Do you look for God's will mainly in the Bible or in the "givens of your being?" (101)

The Ragamuffin Gospel Brennan Manning

1. Is your spirituality more one of personal responsibility or personal response? (17)

2. For the saved sinner . . . and understanding the gospel of grace . . . does repentance come before or after forgiveness? (75)

3. Is your pattern to do the right thing for the right reasons or wrong reasons? (135)

4. Is your "home" a heavenly mansion in the afterlife, or a safe place right in the midst of your anxious world? (John 14:23) (148)

5. Do you see other people as they are or as you are? (157)

6. The question at the core of our ability to mature and grow spiritually: Do you really accept the message that God is head over heels in love with you? (165)

7. What does God say when you tell Him you love Him? Thank you. (166)

8. As we get older, we do only the things we do well (for fear of failure). Agree? (175)

9. Do you try to live so He will love you or do you live because He already loves you? (183)

10. Did Peter ever praise God for the servant girl in Caiaphas' courtyard who turned him into a sniveling coward? (184)

11. What did the Prodigal Father (in effect) say to his son: "Hush, child, I don't need to know where you've been or what you've been up to." (188)

12. Is the general orientation of your life toward peace and joy? (202)

13. Does fear keep you from love? Being loved? (216)

14. What question, in effect, will embody all others God will ask you on Judgment Day? Did you believe that I love you? That I desired you? That I waited for you day after day? (233)

15. Describe not the deity you have heard about or been taught to believe exists, but only the Christ you have actually encountered. (235)

16. The one thing we absolutely owe to God is never to be afraid of anything. (255)

Blue Like Jazz by **Donald Miller**

1. What religious habits do you have that keep your heart from engaging God? (13)

2. When you read of other countries and wars and murders and rapes, do you think you are capable of those? (16)

3. Do you feel more subdued or freer since you came to Christ? (18)

4. Where have you had more significant spiritual experiences.... In church or elsewhere? (42)

5. Christian spirituality: "It cannot be explained, and yet it is beautiful and true. It is something you feel, and it comes from the soul." (57) Agree/disagree?

Searching for God Knows What by **Donald Miller**

1. What are times in your life when you have been most happy? (11)

2. Has God created you in His image, or have you created Him in yours? (20)

3. Do you see Christ in what you read in the Bible, or a mirror image of yourself? (60)

4. Are we supposed to have glory on our own, or get glory from the God who love us? (108)

5. Regarding your favorite teams, do you say WE won and THEY lost? (111)

6. Can you present the "gospel" without mentioning Jesus? (159)

7. Have you in some way reduced Scripture to formula, and a love story to theology, and morality to rules? It is a very different thing to break a rule than it is to cheat on a lover. (184)

Waking the Dead by **John Eldredge**

1. The glory of God is man fully alive (St. Irenaeus). What do you think? (10)

2. Which came first, original sin or original glory? Which is deeper to our nature? (14)

3. What do you dwell on? What controls you?

4. What is the first piece of equipment Paul tells us to put on in Ephesians 6? Belt of truth.

5. Do you feel like you are losing heart? (22)

6. How do efficiency, busyness and productivity crowd out your heart? (38)

7. The seed that falls on good soil stands for those with what kind of heart? Noble and good. (40)

8. Was the cross meant to be the only or central symbol of Christianity? (64)

9. If you KNEW your heart was good, what would happen? How would it change you? (69)

10. Would you say this is true? Christ has come to give you back your heart and set you free. (75)

11. Do you believe God speaks to us personally? "He who belongs to God hears what God says." John 8:47 (102)

12. Do you think your heart is good and that it matters to God? (122)

13. Do you often think in the category of "caring for your heart"? (208)

14. How would you live differently if you believed your heart was the treasure of the kingdom? (210)

15. Caring for your heart is how we begin to love. (211)

16. Is your life ruled by the expectations of others? If so, your heart is always the first thing to go. (216)

The Silence of Adam by **Larry Crabb**

1. Eve was deceived by the snake. Was Adam? No. (11)

2. Does spiritual manhood have more to do with continuing to function in spite of difficulties than with successfully overcoming them? (13)

3. Do you think you have been an imposter most of your life? (19)

4. Where did Adam's disobedience begin? With his silence . . . not his eating. (97)

Healing the Masculine Soul by **Gordon Dalbey**

1. "How is it in America that a boy is called by the men?" Asked by an African villager, referring to initiation. (49)

2. What might an authentic Christian, authentic male initiation look like? (54)

3. Do you fear being strong with your girlfriend/wife for fear she will leave you? (74)

4. In today's marriages, does the least committed one have the most power? (The one most likely to leave.) (85)

5. Fathers and sons may ask each other, "Do you love me?" But the real question they're asking is, "Am I yours? Do you claim me as your own? Do you value me enough to affirm that I am a part of you?" (152)

6. What are you more comfortable with . . . religion or spirituality? Most men choose religion because we are anxious to control what we fear most. (197)

Abba's Child by Brennan Manning

1. We cannot accept love from another human being if we don't . . . love ourselves. (20) Do you?

2. When you see Jesus looking at you, what do you see in His eyes? Good story! (20)

3. Where does the spiritual life begin? With the acceptance of our wounded self. (21)

4. What is Satan's greatest psychological weapon? Low self-esteem. (23)

5. What is the greatest enemy of the spiritual life? Self rejection. (24)

6. Guilt is an idol. Bonhoeffer. (29)

7. Do you like being alone with yourself? Why or why not? Yet this is the self you inflict on others! (23)

8. Do you see the Bible as a love story or a detailed manual of directions? (77)

9. The child spontaneously expresses emotions; the Pharisee carefully represses them. What are you? (88)

Books I Have Enjoyed

Brennan Manning
> *The Ragamuffin Gospel*
> *Ruthless Trust*
> *Abba's Child*

David G. Benner
> *Surrender to Love*
> *The Gift of Being Yourself*
> *Desiring God's Will*

Bill Thrall, Bruce McNicol, John Lynch
> *True Faced*

William Paul Young
> *The Shack*

Brent Curtis & John Eldredge
> *The Sacred Romance*

John Eldredge
> *Wild at Heart*
> *The Way of the Wild Heart (Fathered by God)*
> *Waking the Dead*

Donald Miller
> *Blue Like Jazz*
> *Searching for God Knows What*

22536807R00093

Made in the USA
San Bernardino, CA
11 July 2015